T0084687

BASICS OF SEMIOTICS

Other Books of Interest from St. Augustine's Press

Patrick J. Deneen, *Conserving America?: Essays on Present Discontents*

Roger Kimball, *The Fortunes of Permanence:*
Culture and Anarchy in an Age of Amnesia

David Ramsay Steele, *Orwell Your Orwell: A Worldview on the Slab*

Zbigniew Janowski, *Homo Americanus:*
The Rise of Totalitarian Democracy in America

Taylor F. Flagg (editor), *The Long Night of the Watchman:*
Essays by Václav Benda, 1977–1989

David Lowenthal, *Slave State: Rereading Orwell's 1984*

Daniel J. Mahoney, *Recovering Politics, Civilization, and the Soul:*
Essays on Pierre Manent and Roger Scruton

Allen Mendenhall, *Shouting Softly: Lines on Law, Literature, and Culture*

Paul M. Weyrich, and William S. Lind, *The Next Conservatism*

Rémi Brague, *The Anchors in the Heavens*

Rémi Brague, *Moderately Modern*

Rémi Brague, *On the God of the Christians (and on one or two others)*

Rémi Brague, *The Legitimacy of the Human*

Jeremy Black, *The Importance of Being Poirot*

Jeremy Black, *In Fielding's Wake*

Joseph Bottum, *Spending the Winter*

Josef Pieper, *Traditional Truth, Poetry, Sacrament:*
For My Mother, on her 70th Birthday

Alexandre Kojève, *The Concept, Time, and Discourse*

Gene Fendt, *Camus' Plague: Myth for Our World*

Roger Scruton, *The Politics of Culture and Other Essays*

Roger Scruton, *The Meaning of Conservatism: Revised 3rd Edition*

Roger Scruton, *An Intelligent Person's Guide to Modern Culture*

Winston Churchill, *The River War*

BASICS OF SEMIOTICS
JOHN DEELY

St. Augustine's Press
South Bend, Indiana

©1990 by John Deely

All rights reserved

No part of this book may be reproduced or utilized in any form or
by any means, electronic or mechanical, including photocopying
and recording, or by any information storage and retrieval
system, without permission in writing from the publisher. The
Association of American University Presses' resolution on
Permissions constitutes the only exception to this prohibition.

The paper used in this publication meets the minimum requirements of American
National Standard for Information Sciences—Permanence of Paper for Printed
Library Materials, ANSI Z39.48-1984.

⊗™

Manufactured in the United States of America

Library of Congress Cataloging-in-Publication Data

Deely, John N.
Basics of semiotics / John Deely.
p.   cm. — (Advances in semiotics)
Includes bibliographical references.
ISBN 0-253-31676-6 (alk. paper). — ISBN 0-253-20568-9 (pbk. : alk. paper)
ISBN 13 978-1-58731-061-4 (pbk)
1. Semiotics. I. Title. II. Series.
P99.D398 1990
401'.41—dc20   89-45354
                                                            CIP

4 5 6 7 8 03 02 01 00 99

This book is dedicated to

Brooke Williams
who edited the whole
raising questions as she often answers them
—like bursts of light

and

Ralph Austin Powell
who made the whole theoretically possible
and before that best taught me how to philosophize

CONTENTS

LIST OF ILLUSTRATIONS

Preface

The last half-century or so has witnessed an increasing interest in semiotic inquiry, with a concomitant scholarly production around the world of books, journals, and articles devoted to the endless facets of the subject. The image of astronomy in 1611 conveyed by John Donne has been suggested as the image of the modern semiotic universe: "Tis all in pieces, all coherence gone; / All just supply, and all Relation".

For conspicuously absent in the burgeoning semiotic literature has been a unified treatise laying out the basics behind the very idea of semiotic inquiry in general, a treatise providing a map of semiosis as an integral phenomenon (it being understood that semiosis is but the name for the action of signs, which provides the common subject matter for the whole range of inquiries covered by the umbrella term "semiotics"). This book is a remedy for that absence, a first approximation to a comprehensive rationale for the linking of semiosis at the levels of culture, society, and nature organic and inorganic.

I have tried to have a fair regard for contemporary and historical scholarship, but nothing has been included here just for the sake of being included. I have not followed the practice of allowing the sociological prestige attained by the application of special methods within semiotics, or by celebrated idiosyncratic preoccupations of individual authors, to enter *eo ipso* into the account. I have tried to allow the requirements of the subject matter to dictate the references at every point. So if there are some strange omissions, as may seem, the reader is asked first to entertain the hypothesis that the omissions are due less to ignorance than to the objective of answering the question of what is really basic in the outline of this subject matter. There can be disagreement over basics, but, for the disagreement to be fruitful, someone has first to make a stab at saying what the basics are. Here is my guess at the riddle of how all being "pieces" and "relation" can yet supply a coherence of substance.

The aim of the book, then, is to fill the need for an answer to the question of just what is the essential nature and what are the fundamental varieties of possible semiosis. The substance of the answer to this twofold question is contained in chapters 3 through 6. Corresponding to this answer is the answer in chapter 2 to the prior question of what semiotics itself—the knowledge corresponding to the subject matter—basically is. And bracketing this whole discussion by way of opening and closing is a kind of sociological look at semiotics today in chapter 1, balanced by a historical look at semiotics in retrospect and prospect in chapter 7.

This is a book I have long wanted to write and one that has, for even longer, needed to be written; but, at least for this author, only recently have the essential insight and opportunity come together for expressing in a coherent overall framework the basic concepts of semiotics. I believe the book effectively demonstrates the thesis Sebeok advanced in his 1975 "Chronicle of Prejudices" (156):

> Movement towards the definition of semiotic thinking in the biological and anthropological [and, I would add, physical environmental] framework of a theory of evolution represents . . . the only genuinely novel and significantly wholistic trend in the 20th century development in this field.

The twenty-first century, I hope, will bear this out, and we will see an end to the "sad fact" recorded by Sebeok more recently (1989b: 82)that "the contemporary teaching of semiotics is severely, perhaps cripplingly, impoverished" by "the utter, frightening innocence of most practitioners of semiotics about the natural order in which they and it are embedded." Semiotics indeed "will surely shrivel and wither unless this lesson sinks in", but the optimism and message of this book is that the lesson, being inscribed in the very object of semiotic inquiry, has to sink in as the inquiry continues to be pursued.

Debts in writing a book are normally theoretical or practical. In this case, one debt, like semiotics itself, straddles the two—the work of Brooke Williams in editing the manuscript. The theoretical debts should be clear enough from the references in the text itself and from the dedication. Here I will mention only the main practical debts, after first noting a terminological point that might otherwise cause the English reader some confusion.

This book was conceived and written in Brazil, while I was a visiting professor on the Faculdade de Letras of the Universidade Federal de Minas Gerais in Belo Horizonte (UFMG). In the background to all that is written here is the recurring linguistic problem of the final "s" often added nowadays to the technical term "semiotic". Although English readers tend to take it that way, the "s" on this word is not a plural form, but rather a kind of malformation puristically speaking. Since the malformation is inevitable anyway in popular consciousness, in earlier writing for English-speakers, I have taken the occasion of the linguistic accident of the two forms to convey a difference between foundational and superstructural inquiries in the field.

That strategy is unworkable in Portuguese. There is no way to accommodate the distinction of these two forms ("semiotic" vs. "semiotics") at the level of a single lexical item, because the Portuguese term "semiótica" is required equally for both. To insist in the context of a Portuguese-speaking audience on the form of the distinction as earlier established in English, therefore, would be tantamount to making an at least twofold grammatical accident (first of the peculiar class of "ics" words, second of contemporary popular English) into an obstacle to the effective presentation of the broadest and most fundamental issues.

In the present work, accordingly, an accident of Portuguese has led me to strike a compromise which extricates us from relying overmuch on an accident of English. While I have varied the two forms in context in ways that could be shown to be consistent with earlier specialized discussions in English, I have not made an issue of the two forms in their variation in this work—a variation which disappears in the Portuguese. Instead, my concern in the present work has been, rather, to convey and to establish the overlap and common core in the comprehension of both of the forms as they occur in general use today, and hence to use them even in their difference as suits the conveyance of the single form "semiótica" (or semiotic, or semiotics) for a presentation of the broadest and most fundamental issues leading to an integral *doctrina signorum* today.

In view of the practical circumstances which concretely gave rise to this book, I must thank first of all the members of the Fulbright Commission in the United States, who appointed me to the UFMG, and second of all Dr. Marco Antônio da Rocha, Executive Director of the Fulbright Commission in Brasília, whose decision to extend my appointment for another semester made the completion of the book possible. Along with these gentlemen of the Fulbright Commission I owe thanks to James Barta, President of Loras College in Dubuque, Iowa, for the leave of absence to work in Brazil.

The chapters of the book reflect my work in semiotics particularly since the publication of *Introducing Semiotic* in 1982. The present book ends by confirming with new detail the outline for a history of semiotic inquiry with which that book began. Williams (1985a: xxvi) has made the point that the synchronic and diachronic, being mutually implicatory at all points, can be "distinguished but not separated in semiosis". In just such a way does the overall perspective of the two works differ, that of the earlier book emphasizing diachrony, whereas a synchronic overview of the general theoretical possibilities for semiotic research dominates the present book throughout. *Introducing Semiotic* lent to the past a shape from the present toward shaping the future. *Basics of Semiotics* gives the full proportions of that mediating shape.

In particular, the chapters of this book reflect mainly the two courses and eight lectures I gave in Brazil during the winter semester of 1988. Chapters 1, 3, and 4 reflect the plenary address and "short course" given at the VII Seminário Internacional de Semiótica e Literatura at Campina Grande in Paraíba on September 19 and September 20–22. I thank Professoras Elizabeth Marinheiro and Celina Alves Pereira who arranged the invitation.

Chapter 2 is one of two partial exceptions to the Brazilian pattern of the whole. For this chapter my main thanks go to Professor Desmond Fitz-Gerald of the University of San Francisco, who brought the thoughts there expressed into their first rough form through the invitation he arranged for me to address, on May 29, 1987, a Language Colloquium being held at his university. These ideas were further refined in classroom and informal discussions at the UFMG in my course on the development of semiotic consciousness, but the original draft was made in San Francisco.

Chapter 5, the other partial exception, is substantially drawn from an article now in press with *The American Journal of Semiotics* under the title "Sign, Text, and Criticism as Elements of Anthroposemiosis". Besides being a distillation of the text used for my course at the UFMG on language from a semiotic point of view, putting flesh on the bones of the integral model for human experience outlined in *Introducing Semiotic*, Part II, Section 3, and again in the editors' preface to *Frontiers in Semiotics*, subsequent drafts of this distillation were criticized editorially and much improved through the suggestions of Brooke Williams, Floyd Merrell, Myrdene Anderson, and Dean MacCannell. To these four editors are due thanks for this chapter.

Chapter 6 reflects in particular ideas presented at the Pontificia Universidade Católica de São Paulo in a long lecture delivered on November 23. My thanks to Professora Maria Lúcia Santaella Braga, who arranged the lecture and provided incomparable hospitality for me and my wife and who, by her enthusiasm alone, persuaded my audience that the idea of a semiosis affecting even the stars might be of value.

Chapter 7 reflects particularly the Ciclo de Conferências I gave at the Universidade de Brasília, November 16–18. My thanks to Professor Karl Erik Schollhammer, who arranged the conferences, and who inspired, in the course of his own class lecture that I attended on Jakobson's poetics, the formulation of the peculiarly semiotic integration of history and theory expressed here. Karl Erik's hospitality and conversations were of exceptional value in gestating this work.

I thank Professor Myrdene Anderson of Purdue University, Professor Nathan Houser of the Peirce Edition Project at Indiana University–Purdue University at Indianapolis, and Professor Ralph McInerny of Notre Dame University for the help they provided from afar in nailing down a few key references.

Over and above the specific work on the volume, thanks go to the faculty members of the Departamento de Letras Germânicas of the UFMG for their friendliness to me and their interest in semiotics. These thanks are due to the Chefe in particular, Professora Stela Beatris Tôrres Arnold, who arranged the details of my stay with the faculty. I thank Professora Ana Lúcia Almeida Gazolla, Pró-Reitora de Pós-Graduação da UFMG, for her early suggestion of the extension of my stay.

Special thanks go to Professora Júnia de Castro Magalhães Alves for her careful readings of the chapters and general interest in the progress of the work and for the countless ways in which she helped two strangers become at home in a new language and land. She also embodied the healthy skepticism that should seize any reader confronting a first "volume of basics". When I told her the third chapter was complete, she answered "Yes. But is it any good?" Now the question applies to the whole.

Thanks go to the students who, by their attendance in the courses and their discussions, concretely demonstrated interest in our subject matter— which is the essential encouragement for any professor. Among these students, two stand out in the intelligence of their enthusiasm: Thaïs Flores Nogueira Diniz and Júlio César Jeha. Senhor Jeha also helped directly in preparing the bibliography for this work, and in providing a first draft for the translation of chapter 5.

I thank J. Bantim Duarte, Editorial Director of Editora Ática in São Paulo, for extending a contract for the work in Portuguese translation; and Professora Ana Cláudia de Oliveira for her linguistic support in bringing that November 25 meeting in the Ática offices to its successful conclusion.

An acknowledgement goes above all to my colleague Julio C. M. Pinto, who was himself on the Paraiba program and provided the translation for my lectures there. Out of that collaboration grew the concrete proposal that became this book. His translation of the whole into Portuguese for Editora Ática is my deepest source of debt in making of this Brazilian book a reality for readers in Brazil.

JOHN DEELY
Belo Horizonte
29 May 1989

BASICS OF SEMIOTICS

"A sign is an objective cause, not the principal objective cause, but a substitutive one, by reason of which a sign is said to be instrumental, not indeed as if it were an instrument of an acting agent, but as it is a substitute for an object, not informing as a specifying form, but representing from outside what it represents."

"An object in general . . . consists in this, that it be something extrinsic, from which derives and upon which depends the intrinsic rationale and specific character of any capacity or act; and this is reduced to the category of an extrinsic formal cause not causing existence, but specification."

"If therefore an end as end specifies, it takes on the rationale of an object, for the rationale of a specifying object is one thing, the rationale of a moving end quite another. And thus specification pertains to the order of an extrinsic formal cause; the impetus of an end, to the finalization moving to produce a thing in being. But to move relative to the act of being and existence is outside the order of specification."

John Poinsot 1632a: 195/23–29, 166/4–10 & 177/8–178/7

"It seems a strange thing, when one comes to ponder over it, that a sign should leave its interpreter to supply a part of its meaning; but the explanation of the phenomenon lies in the fact that the entire universe—not merely the universe of existents, but all that wider universe, embracing the universe of existents as a part . . . — . . . is perfused with signs, if it is not composed exclusively of signs."

Charles Sanders Peirce 1905–1906: 5.448n.

"Hence the name of this type of causality is 'extrinsic formal causality'. It is *formal* causality because it specifies the . . . relation, and it is *extrinsic* formal causality because the specifiers lie outside the . . . relation." And they need not exist.

Ralph Austin Powell 1986: 297 & viva voce

1

LITERARY SEMIOTICS AND THE DOCTRINE OF SIGNS

IN THE United States, in contrast with the predominantly literary and linguistic development semiotics has undergone in the more typically European contexts, the development of semiotics has taken a rather different turn, influenced especially perhaps by Thomas A. Sebeok and the many projects associated with the Research Center for Language and Semiotic Studies which he chaired at the Bloomington campus of Indiana University. This development shows promise of providing for the semiotics movement as a whole a new and larger framework for the conduct of research, one that is, to tell the truth, more in keeping with the possibilities contained in Locke's original adumbration of the place of semiotics among the sciences, natural and human alike.

It helps often to have a label identifying important differences, and in this case the labels have largely been provided by the developments themselves. All that is needed is to pluck from the tree of established usages the terms most fruitful for conveying the flavor of the paradigm shift semiotics continues to undergo sociologically, as it expands outward from the literary and the linguistic to take in further the realm of biological forms and, indeed, evolutionary development in general. For the very emergence of semiotic animals is already itself a thirdness respecting the general development of the physical universe. What these terms are was suggested in the French context by Georges Mounin, inadvertently and in spite of himself, as early as 1970 (57n.): "the term semiotic has made its way into

French . . . as a designation for semiology in general—an ill-advised usage. . . ."

What I want to bring out are the underlying reasons why Mounin experienced the emerging usage as "ill-advised", and, at the same time, paradoxically, I want to point out that what was ill-advised was not the emergence of the new usage, but the attempt to equate it with the established usage whereby the designation "semiology" had come to stand for a part mistaken for the whole prospective of a doctrine of signs. From the point of view of the North American development, it turns out to have been profoundly misleading for Decio Pignatari (1971: 27) to announce: "In Europe, Semiotics is called Semiology . . . ."

Asa Berger correctly noted (1982: 14, 17) that "the essential breakthrough of semiology is to take linguistics as a model and apply linguistic concepts to other phenomena—texts—and not just to language itself". So far so good. But if that be the case, then the essential breakthrough of semiotics, by contrast, is to see that the phenomenon of semiosis requires a model within which linguistic phenomena taken together appear as a subset of a much broader range of sign-activity which cannot even be confined to the cultural side of the line defining our ideas of the natural world. In other words, if semiology is rightly taken as a proper name for the genre of semiotics studying the sign as "first of all a construct", in the exact expression of Paul Perron (1983: 1), then semiotics by rights should be taken inclusively to name that larger realm of which semiology forms but a distinguished part, including, as it does in anthroposemiosis, the highest achievements of semiosis, undoubtedly literary.

What I would like to do here, then, is suggest a way of broadening the consideration of literary semiotics to include in some sense natural phenomena as well as purely cultural and literary texts. Thereby we may see if the notion of narrative as semiotically conceived might not recapture something of the classical philosophical understanding that saw cultural phenomena—including literature—as in some sense an extension of and linked with a larger world of nature which cultural beings no doubt may take for granted and even ignore in their round of life, but which remains nonetheless the inevitable context in which they move and on which they depend even as cultural. For it is this larger ambience which provides in the first place the materials or, as we may say, the raw possibilities of cultural creations—including literary texts, just as it subsequently provides for their sustenance.

In his 1984 International Summer Institute for Semiotic and Structural Studies (ISISSS) workshop on "Semiosis as a Psychologically Embodied Phenomenon", Gary Shank proposed for semiotics the notion of narrative which I would like to make the center of my reflections here. Human beings, he suggested, "are essentially narrative as opposed to the other animals." This is an interesting notion and a highly semiotic one. We hear much of formal and logical structures in the context of semiotics. Yet the essential transmission of culture to children takes place first of all under the guise of stories—that is to say, narrative. The animals other than human do not do this. They do not bring their young up on stories, but on instinct and examples—examples of a straight behavioral kind, not examples of heroism or adventure embodied in narrative tales such as sustain the cultures of humankind and constitute the substance of the encultura- tion of children in all societies. We (perhaps the literary semioticians above all) have to face the question raised by Jerome Bruner in his first class of that 1984 ISISSS (May 31): "Why can children understand stories so much earlier than logic?"

Anthropologists bring to our attention rich and exotic data that simi- larly attest to the importance of narrative among all the peoples of the earth. It can perhaps be said that the first of the narrative universals we ought to consider, therefore, is the universal role of narrative as the root of the transmission of culture—the root, as Brooke Williams points out in her essay on history and semiotic (1985), of the distinctively human semiosis whereby biological heredity is transcended in the cumulative transmission of learning that narrative alone makes possible.

From this point of view, a number of clarifications become possible that are of the first importance for semiotics itself in defining its own future and in seizing on the unique opportunities opened up by the development in our day of the doctrine of signs. For the first time in perhaps three hun- dred years, semiotic makes possible the establishment of new foundations for the human sciences, foundations making possible in turn a new super- structure for the humanities and the so-called hard or natural sciences alike. Such a framework has been often dreamed of, but semiotics for the first time puts it within our reach, provided only that we have an under- standing of the sign and its essential functionings sufficiently rich to pre- vent closing off semiotic research within the sphere of constructed signs.

In this regard, the actual development of semiotics in our time pro- vides a number of clues that should not be neglected in our attempts to interpret what sort of human phenomenon we are dealing with. "While every contributor to *Semiotica*", Thomas Sebeok pointed out in 1971 (56), "may indulge his personal taste when attaching a label to the theory of signs", the terminology within the same piece of discourse will not oscillate ad libitum, for the "initial selection will have signaled" to the sophisticated readership the tradition with which the author in question stands princi- pally aligned.

It is well known that semiotics as we find it today traces back mainly to two contemporaneous pioneers, one in the field of linguistics and one in the field of philosophy. The first of these, Ferdinand de Saussure, envi- sioned the possible developments under the label of semiology, which seems to have been a word of his own coining, fashioned, of course, from the Greek *seméion*. The second, C. S. Peirce, chose the name semiotic, also fashioned from the Greek but not of Peirce's own coining. Peirce derived his vision of the possible development we now see being actualized, as he himself tells us, from the text with which John Locke concludes his *Essay Concerning Human Understanding*.

For Saussure, the "science" of signs was to be a branch of social psychology and linguistics a subspecies within that branch, albeit the most important one. Of this "possible science", of course, Saussure himself did not say a great deal. But he did wisely caution that, "since it does not yet exist, one cannot say what form it will take" (i.1906–1911: 33)—a wise caution largely ignored, it must be said, by even the most brilliant of those in our own day who took their early inspiration from Saussure and proceeded to develop a "science" of signs centered exclusively on literary texts and other artifacts of culture, which were always treated on the patterns of language and almost as of a piece with it. Within this tradition, the possibilities of semiotic understanding, though very rich and diversified, have always been restricted in highly artificial ways in terms of what Paul Bouissac, among others, has repeatedly pointed out (for example, 1979, 1981) as glottocentrism.

To this extent, semiotic development has undoubtedly been hampered in establishing the perspective fully proper to itself by some inevitable entanglement with the coils of modern philosophy—the work of the Kantian critiques, in particular, according to which there is no world known or knowable beyond the phenomena constructed by the understanding itself according to its own hidden mechanisms and ineluctable laws. Writing within this tradition, Terence Hawkes (1977: 18) reminds us that:

> It follows that the ultimate quarry of structuralist thinking will be the permanent structures into which individual human acts, perceptions, stances fit, and from which they derive their final nature. This will finally involve what Fredric Jameson has described as [1972: 209] 'an explicit search for the permanent structures of the mind itself, the organizational categories and forms through which the mind is able to experience the world, or to organize a meaning in what is in itself essentially meaningless'.

This tradition, as I have noted, originally flourished under the banner of semiology, a term that today remains far from desuetude. It has, however, been greatly and increasingly influenced in recent years by the other semiotic tradition, which develops not from Saussure but from Peirce and Morris and a number of scientific workers. It does not seem too much to say that, under the pressures of this influence, we have witnessed the coming into being, alongside the term *sémiologie*, the newer term *sémiotique*, a term which, without displacing "sémiologie" entirely, has come to dominate over it and, to a certain extent, replace it, without, however, so far removing the intractable bias toward glottocentrism and philosophical idealism that characterized semiotic development in the Romance areas.

This bias and developing influence, of course, is by no means restricted to the Romance areas. Within current philosophy, David Clarke (1987: 8; cf. 120–121, 137, and *passim*) has made a belated attempt to define semiotic itself in the restrictive terms already established as proper to semiology: an "attempt to extend analogically features initially arrived at by examining language use to more primitive signs, with logical features of language becoming the archetype on which analysis of these latter signs is developed". It is simply a misnomer to title a book based on such a thesis *Principles of Semiotic*. To try to reduce semiotic to the status of a subalternate discipline within the dimensions of current linguistic philosophy already evinces adherence to the modern perspectives of idealism which semiotics points beyond.

Among modern philosophers, the one who struggled most against the coils of idealism and in the direction of a semiotic was Martin Heidegger. His failure to free himself from the modern logocentrism is, to be sure, a testimony to its pervasiveness in modern culture, and to the scale of the task semiotic in its fullest possibilities has to face. Yet in the debate between realism and idealism, he is the one who perhaps most clearly brought to the fore the fact that (1927: 207), whatever its drawbacks and "no matter how contrary and untenable it may be in its results", idealism "has an advantage in principle" over realism. That advantage lies in the simple fact that whenever we observe anything, that observation already presupposes and rests within a semiosis whereby the object observed came to exist as object—that is to say, as perceived, experienced, or known—in the first place.

No one, including Heidegger, realizes this fact better than the semiotician. Indeed, at the heart of semiotics is the realization that the whole of human experience, without exception, is an interpretive structure mediated and sustained by signs. So it is perhaps not surprising that much of the original semiotic development in our time has taken place along the tracks and lines of a classical idealism in the modern sense, an environment and climate of thought within which the structuralist analysis of texts and narratives is particularly comfortable.

Yet we are entitled to wonder if such a perspective is enough to allow for the full development of the possibilities inherent in the notion of a doctrine of signs—to wonder if the "way of signs" does not lead outside of and well beyond the classical "way of ideas" of which Locke also spoke. We are entitled to wonder if what we need is not rather, as the recent collaborative monograph by Anderson et al. calls for (1984: 1), "a semiotics which provides the human sciences with a context for reconceptualizing foundations and for moving along a path which, demonstrably, avoids crashing headlong into the philosophical roadblock thrown up by forced choices between realism and idealism, as though this exclusive dichotomy were also exhaustive of the possibilities of interpreting human experience".

Such a development seems to be what is taking place in the tradition of semiotic. This tradition, in fact, given its name by Locke, had reached the level of explicit thematic consciousness and systematically unified expression only very late—as far as we currently know, not before the *Tractatus de Signis* essayed in 1632 by the Iberian philosopher of Portuguese birth, John Poinsot (Sebeok 1982; Deely 1988). But, as Sebeok remarks (1976: 1), what we are faced with, under many different names fragmented by the perspectives from which those names spring, is "an ancient discipline" developing through many channels and byways toward the era of its full thematic systematization and baptism under its own name and according to the perspective proper to itself. For this same discipline *in nuce*— semiotic as the doctrine of signs—is discernible in the most ancient origins of Greek medicine, philosophy, and linguistic reflections, as recent work has begun to exhibit (Romeo 1976, 1977, 1979; Deely 1982, 1985; Eco and Deely 1983; Eco 1984; Eschbach and Trabant 1983; Doyle 1984).

This tradition of Poinsot-Locke-Peirce, unlike that of Saussure, does not take its principal and almost exclusive inspiration from human language and speech. It sees in semiosis a broader and much more fundamental process, involving the physical universe itself in human semiosis, and making of semiosis in our species a part of semiosis in nature. Abduction, the process whereby alone new ideas are seized upon—ideas further to be developed deductively and tested inductively, beginning again the cycle, or, rather, spiral (Deely 1985a: figure 2; 1985b)—is first of all a phenomenon of nature. It works with constructed signs, but not only with constructed signs, and not with constructed signs first of all.

We have here two traditions or paradigms, which have to a certain extent handicapped the contemporary development by existing within it under sociological conditions of opposition, an opposition not only uncalled for logically, but one which depends on a perverse synecdoche where a part is mistaken for the whole. Semiotics forms a whole of which semiology is but a part.

Let me try to clarify the relationship by applying a linguistic metaphor. Philosophers of Latin times made the distinction between what they called *ens reale* and *ens rationis* a staple of their discourse, and they assigned in general a very clear sense to this dichotomy. They nowhere took effective notice, however, of the fact that the so-called beings of reason have a kind of reality in their own right, and that there is something curious about a distinction so drawn that one of its terms includes the other—something that requires further explanation. From the standpoint of human experience, the greater part of what we call culture, also social roles, is constituted precisely by so-called beings of reason. And, finally, there is the fact that, from this same standpoint, "reality"—what we experience directly in everyday life—is a mixture irreducible to so-called *ens reale*.

Certainly the themes and objects of what I have here called "semiology", that is, the texts and themes of literature and language-constituted phenomena generally, belong to the order of *entia rationis* in the Latin sense. But, in the Latin sense, this object domain was also shown to be dependent upon a larger whole and ordered to that larger whole—namely, the universe of nature as we experience it. As autonomous, the sphere of human culture is but *relatively* autonomous, as transcending, but only by incorporating and resting upon, a physical environment shared with all the forms of biological life in a larger network—biosemiosis—of mutual dependence. The understanding of that larger whole precisely in terms of semiosis defines the complete task of which cultural semiotics forms a part.

The perspective of semiotic is the perspective in which "real being" and "being of reason" come together, not the perspective in which they are opposed. As John Poinsot, the first semiotician to thematize this point, put it (1632a: 118/2–6):

> We are discussing the sign in general, as it includes equally the natural and the social sign, in which perspective even those signs which are mental artifacts—namely, stipulated signs as such—are involved.

Poinsot's original point has also been restated in the terms of a contemporary semiotician. Human evolution, Sebeok tells us (1977: 182–183), is

> not only a reconfirmation of the evolutionary processes which went on before man appeared on the scene, but continues as a dual semiotic consecution that can scarcely be uncoupled in practice: one track language-free (or zoosemiotic), the other language-sensitive (or anthroposemiotic). Semiosis must be recognized as a pervasive fact of nature as well as of culture.

Within this framework, Sebeok (1984a: 3) reminds us, the tradition of semiology is a subordinate part in relation to semiotics to the extent that semiology is fixed upon "that minuscule segment of nature some anthropologists grandly compartmentalize as culture."

Let me cite Sebeok's original description of terms on this theme of the two traditions (1977: 181ff.):

> The chronology of semiotic inquiry so far, viewed panoramically, exhibits an oscillation between two seemingly antithetical tendencies: in the major tradition (which I am tempted to christen a Catholic heritage), semiosis takes its place as a normal occurrence of nature, of which, to be sure, language— that paramount known mode of terrestrial communication which is La-

marckian in style, that is, embodies a learning process that becomes part of the evolutionary legacy of the ensuing generations—forms an important if relatively recent component. . . .

The minor trend, which is parochially glottocentric, asserts, sometimes with sophistication but at other times with embarrassing naivete, that linguistics serves as the model for the rest of semiotics—Saussure's *le patron générale*—because of the allegedly arbitrary and conventional character of the verbal sign.

This theme of "the two traditions" is one that needs to be developed very carefully if it is to be rightly understood. It is not at all a matter of "two traditions": one ('Anglo-Saxon') arising from Peirce, the other ('Continental') arising from Saussure, which "seem to have developed separately and without interpenetration", as Parret erroneously asserts (1984: 220). Such an assertion is true neither sociologically nor theoretically. Nor is it a matter (Watt 1984: 104, 106, glossing Percival 1981) of Saussure's "long-term position in semiotic history, and his present utility", on the ground that "almost everything that is based on Saussure can just as well be based on older sources, and nothing is lost by doing so". Still less is it a question of whether (ibid.: 130, glossing Atkins 1981) "Derrida has not unseated 2000 years of 'Western metaphysics': at most he has (unwittingly) exposed a few of Saussure's inadequacies, a very different matter."

What is at issue simply is the intent and scope of the term semiotic as Locke introduced it, and of the notion of "reality" as the perspective Locke labelled opens unto it (Deely 1986b). The "major and minor traditions", rightly understood, are no more opposed than are "ens reale and ens rationis" in the perspective proper to a doctrine of signs.[1] It is not a relation of exclusion that obtains but a relation of part to whole—and of a *pars pro toto fallacy* that prevails when proponents of the part mistake it for or try to set it in opposition to the whole.

If in Europe, as we have seen Pignatari allege (1971: 27), "semiotics is called semiology", we see that, in Europe, something false is directly spoken, but something true is also indirectly spoken and through a metonymy. Inheritors of the Iberian university traditions, both Portuguese and Spanish, are in a privileged position to contribute to this truth, through a recapturing and making vital to the contemporary development of semiotic of the reflections on the sign undertaken by their own thinkers between Ockham and Descartes.

---

1. The first anthology or 'reader' to attempt to define the current situation from this point of view, *Frontiers in Semiotics* (Deely, Williams, and Kruse 1986), is built on the advice of Margaret Mead (1964: 287): "In this situation"—to wit, the establishment of semiotics among the traditional specialized perspectives of the sciences and humanities—"cooperation is the crucial condition for success."

2

SEMIOTICS: METHOD OR POINT OF VIEW?

SEMIOTICS HAS given rise to a variety of methods. No doubt this variety, already considerable, is bound to increase under the ingenuity of the growing band of semiotic workers.

But the question is whether semiotics as a whole *consists* in or can be identified with such methods. The question is whether, in coming into its own, semiotics will continue modern philosophy's obsession with method or will establish its theoretical framework with sufficient richness and flexibility to accommodate itself to the full range of signifying phenomena. Will semiotics, in other words, develop the full variety and flexibility of methods that an eventual understanding of these phenomena will evoke?

A method, after all, implements some aspect or aspects of a point of view; indeed, the systematic implementation of something suggested by a point of view is pretty much what a method is. But a point of view that can be fully implemented by a single method would be, on the whole, a very narrow viewpoint. The richer a point of view, the more diverse are the methods needed to exploit the possibilities for understanding latent within it.

This distinction between *method* and *point of view*, therefore, is actually a rather important one. It is like the distinction within logic between extension and comprehension: without the latter, the former would not be possible.

Modern philosophy was characterized by a search for a method. Descartes searched for an introspective method that could yield certainty at the foundation of the sciences. Leibniz searched for a calculatory method for resolving all the problems of philosophy, particularly those that had a bearing on religion and theological dispute. Spinoza sought a geometric method applicable to ethical discussion. Newton sought a mathematical method for interpreting the details of nature. And so on.

I came to think, in my own study of philosophy, that the search for *a* method was in a certain sense modern philosophy's failure. So engrossed were the moderns by their search for the one true method that they overlooked, in their very assumption of it, the perspective common to all of them that guided their search to begin with and, at the same time, made it futile. The one thread that unified the modern philosophers to me was the fact that they each began with the assumption that our ideas represent themselves.[2] These philosophers ended unable to explain and absolutely baffled by how we could know anything besides our own ideas, since ideas so construed are each one's own, that is to say, private, ideas.

The situation created by this presupposition was systematized by Immanuel Kant, especially in his *Critique of Pure Reason* (1781, 1787) but also in the whole set of the *Critiques*. What Kant did was to systematize the modern conundrum in such a way that, while communication as a true sharing of insight is absolutely impossible within the Kantian system, the appearance of communication can be sustained by the fact that the a–priori mechanisms of our sense and understanding are specifies-specific and as such the same in each of us. Thus, it can seem that we are communicating even though in reality the communication appearing to occur is impossible.

And this is not so different from the situation hypothecated by Leibniz, who explained communication ultimately through the hookup of the individual monads with the Divine Monad, the great communications satellite in the sky that made my representations correspond with yours and so on for every other creature forming and projecting its own private representations.

Now I say, in contrast with all of this, that semiotics provides not a method first of all but a point of view. From within this point of view it becomes clear that ideas are not self-representations but signs of what is objectively other than and superordinate to the idea in its being as a private representation. Semiotic is a perspective or a point of view that arises from an explicit recognition of what every method of thought or every research method presupposes. Semiotic arises from the attempt to make thematic this ground that is common to all methods and sustains them transparently

---

2. That is to say, in our terms, that our ideas are in the first place objects rather than signs. How this seemingly innocent assumption conflicts with and impacts upon the possibilities of semiotic understanding of conceptions and experience we will see at some length in chapter 5.

throughout to the extent that they are genuine means by which inquiry is advanced. Semiotics, then, or the semiotic point of view, rests on the realization of a unique form of activity in nature, as we will look at in some detail in the chapters following, and for which, as we have seen, Charles Sanders Peirce coined the name *semiosis*.

This activity, the action of signs, is in fact presupposed by the very idea of method. Signs, that is to say, are required not only for any given method in philosophy or in the sciences, natural or human, but for the very possibility of there being such a thing as method or inquiry of any kind. Semiosis is a process of revelation, and every process of revelation involves in its very nature the possibility of deceit or betrayal. Every method reveals something (hence some truth about the world, some aspect of the world, or some field of investigation), and, insofar as it reveals, is a semiotic method, by which I mean simply that it is, as a communicative modality, something sign-dependent.

Conversely, any method ceases to be semiotic only as and insofar as it betrays its character as a method, by treating the signs upon which it relies as if they were merely objects. So we have bizarre methods, for example, in the recent history of philosophy, such as logical positivism, with its so-called verification theory of meaning, put forward as a means of removing nonsense from philosophy, by a twofold (and doubly arbitrary) stipulation telescoping the signification of dicisigns[3] into their truth and further telescoping their truth into the sense-perceptible dimension or aspect as such of their signifieds. Thus, only a dicisign designating sensibly accessible significates could be true, and only true designations of such signifieds could have significance.

No sooner was this method announced than it was rightly denounced as a sham, on patent and blatant grounds that verification presupposes signification, for what cannot be understood can be neither proved (verified) nor disproved. This circularity made the ballyhooed method in fact untenable from the beginning. After more than a quarter of a century of beating around the bush on the point, we find such "greats" of the positivist era as A. J. Ayer informing us that, after all, the verification theory of meaning must be somewhat modified. In order to verify a proposition, the proposition must first be understood. But, if it can be understood independently of being verified, it must have some other "meaning" than that which depends directly on verification—some meaning, indeed, that makes verifi-

---

3. *Dicisigns* or "propositions", that is to say, signs that both represent and make an assertion, positive or negative, about what is represented, in contrast both to *represigns*, "rhemes", or "terms" (isolated linguistic elements whether simple or complex that represent without asserting anything about what is represented) and to *suadisigns* or "arguments" (complex linguistic forms that give reasons for accepting or rejecting something asserted about what they represent). This terminology taken from Peirce I expand and develop in full in a book now almost complete, *Logic within Semiotics* (Indiana University Press, forthcoming).

cation thinkable and possible in the first place. This objection had been stated already in the first week of the debate, and hardly needed Ayer's belated acknowledgment to stick. (Indeed, what calls for explanation is the belatedness of the acknowledgment.)

So the verification theory, though paraded as a method for eliminating as "nonsense" metaphysical concerns from science and from philosophy itself, was rather a method for replacing philosophical questions with ideological commitments disguised as philosophy. The verification theory, in short, insofar as it involved a method, did exactly what any method does: it implemented a theory and point of view—in this case, a dogmatic and ideological one hostile to philosophical tradition and incapable of considering its own foundations without becoming internally inconsistent: a sorry approach indeed. The root incompatibility of the ideology behind the method with a semiotic point of view was already a primary sign of this antinomy at the foundations of the verification theory of meaning. The same would have to be said for Bertrand Russell's so-called "Theory of Descriptions" within logic, or B. F. Skinner's so-called "Behaviorism" (after Watson, for whom, unlike Sherlock Holmes' companion, consciousness counted for nothing): these "methods" did not merely implement a point of view, but paraded the point of view itself in the guise of a method, thereby objectifying the sign processes on which they relied in such a way as to make it appear, or at least enable one to pretend, that no other point of view on the objects considered could have legitimacy.

I distinguish then, first of all, a point of view from a method, and I want to say that semiotics, like logical positivism or behaviorism, is a point of view rather than a method. But, at the same time, unlike positivism or behaviorism, *semiotics* in its doctrinal foundation is not an ideological standpoint that can be disguised as a method of inquiry while in reality closing inquiry down.

While we can make the objection that, in practice, semiotics can *never* be ideologically free, as all semioticians as human inquirers hold some ideological stance, the point remains that any such ideological stance, however intrinsic to semioticians' understandings of "semiotics", is nonetheless *extrinsic* to the doctrine of signs, which does not in itself prescribe a given ideology disguised as a method of inquiry. Semiotics rather depends upon the maintaining of a point of view, which not only is transdisciplinary but also is in a basic sense presupposed to and therefore compatible with every method insofar as the method truly reveals something of the world or of the nature of the subject matter into which it inquires, including the arteriosclerotic ideologies confused with methods. That is to say (since even bad methods truly reveal), the compatibility of semiotics according to what is proper to it as realizing the role of the sign in every method is its capacity for revealing in the method what that method conceals as well as what it discloses—that is to say, the abiding difference between a method as implementing a point of view and the point of view itself implemented. In this way, a semiotic standpoint is able to reveal when *too much has been excluded*, as is always the case to the extent that an ideological stance is being concealed *in the guise of* a "method".

To be ideological and to be historically conditioned, therefore, are not necessarily the same. The latter is true of every attempt at inquiry, including semiotics. The former is true of semiotics only to the extent that and whenever the perspective proper to the sign is traded for something else in the subjectivity of the inquirer. But then this trade will inevitably reveal itself objectively in the public deployment of consequent sign-systems (for example, in the speech or writing of the inquirer), where it will become visible to others in the community of inquirers and subject to criticism with appropriate revision or rejection.

Thus, even the "method of verification", like the "method of dialectics", had need of some signs in order to deny other signs. Its illegitimacy lay not in the signs it used but in the signs it refused, to wit, the signs that would have carried the discourse beyond the arbitrarily stipulated boundaries and were covertly relied upon in order to assert the illegitimate boundaries in the first place.

What, then, are we to say the semiotic point of view is? And how is it that this point of view, unlike others, cannot properly be reduced to or converted into an ideology? To answer the questions in order: The semiotic point of view is the perspective that results from the sustained attempt to live reflectively with and follow out the consequences of one simple realization: the whole of our experience, from its most primitive origins in sensation to its most refined achievements of understanding, is a network or web of sign relations. This point of view cannot be reduced to an ideology without losing what is proper to it for the reason that its boundaries are those of the understanding itself in its activity of interpreting dependently upon the cognate interpretations of perception and sensation.

Since this network, which when brought to light through reflection establishes a novel perspective, is first of all a matter of experience, in this book we will stick strictly to the basics. We will begin at precisely that point where semiotics, in its contrast with semiosis—that is to say, as a thematically unified and organic network of knowledge—becomes possible, namely, in the reflective experience of linguistic animals. We will see that the origin of semiotics and the drawing of the line between human and other animals are of a piece, and that, at the same time, the origin of semiotics as the perspective proper to experience by that very fact extends the prospective knowledge semiotics entails beyond the biological boundaries of specifically human animals to encompass all those communicative modalities upon which the deployment and sustenance of specifically linguistic competence depend. Such communicative modalities begin with the obvious involvement of perceptual and sensory modalities hardly uniquely human but include ultimately too the physical environs that sustain these and further communicative modalities beyond the boundaries of what is sensible according to some given biological heritage.

The detailed extensions of semiotics to the living sphere as a whole, and beyond it to inorganic nature, are not matters of common experience ("cenoscopic") but rather matters that depend once formulated on experimental scientific designs for their establishment. As such, they exceed the province of this book, and are left for other works. Here I attempt only a sketch of the foundations and framework which make such detailed extensions feasible. It seems to me, as it seemed to Peirce (1908b: 8.343), "that one of the first useful steps toward a science of *semeiotic* [as he generally misspelled the term taken from Locke], or the cenoscopic science of signs, must be the accurate definition, or logical analysis, of the concepts of the science." After all, if the basics are grounded well and firmly grasped, their extensions and applications will result inevitably in the course of time.

The basic perspective these chapters aim to establish, then, is the perspective proper to the sign according to the being and activity it reveals in the experience of each of us. As virtual to all experience, the actual perspective in question is, therefore, testable analytically by each reader. Moreover, it is rooted first of all in common experience, precisely as that experience reveals itself as a constructed network built over time both through the biological heritage of the animal species as such (in our case, the species *homo sapiens*) and through the individual experiences whereby, atop the biological heritage, socialization and enculturation transpire. The basics of semiotics are a question, in the terms Peirce appropriated from Bentham (1816; see Peirce c.1902a: 1.241–242), of *cenoscopic* rather than *idioscopic* development, that is, they concern layman and specialist alike, and not specialists first of all.

A favorite metaphor, which I got from Sebeok (1975), and which I think he himself got from Jakob von Uexküll,[4] is the metaphor for experience as whole as a semiotic web. We are all familiar at least a little bit with spiders and how they spin their webs and with what these webs do, namely, selectively trap other beings in the environment for the benefit and sustenance of the spider (which is why an ideology is the semiotic equivalent of reducing the human *Lebenswelt* to the praeter-human lines of an *Umwelt*, as we will see in chapter 5). Of course, the scheme sometimes backfires, as I once had occasion to observe. I was standing in the dining room of Stonecliffe Hall looking out into a small rock garden thinking of these matters when a spider happened to descend into my field of

---

4. "As the spider spins its threads, every subject spins his relations to certain characters of the things around him, and weaves them into a firm web which carries his existence" (J. von Uexküll 1934: 14).

vision on a lengthening silken cord that was intended to be one among the several already drawn threads of a nascent web. As the animal descended, a sudden gust of wind nudged the spider sideways into a tangle with already drawn strands from which the spider proved unable to escape, as I learned from the spider's eventual death in the tangle. So this matter of spinning webs is not without an element of danger.

There are many approximations in the history of science and philosophy to the semiotic point of view. One of the easiest ways to approach the whole subject, indeed, is to trace historically these approximations and developments, as I have sometimes tried to do. Here I want to leave any historical observations to a later, subsidiary point in our study (chapter 7), in order to try to explain directly and with some exactness what this semiotic point of view is and how it develops into a perspective compassing the whole of our knowledge and belief and experience of reality.

One of the richest and fullest contemporary approximations to the semiotic point of view is the movement that is known today as hermeneutics. Springing again from the Continent (like rationalism and phenomenology, which it extends), this movement has come to challenge within philosophy the dominance of so-called linguistic analysis or linguistic philosophy in our universities. Important as it is (and I think it is very important), it yet belongs to what was characterized in chapter 1 as the "minor tradition" within semiotics proper. "Semiotics proper" is identified with the point of view here being explained as compassing the prospective whole of experience and therefore the "major tradition" of intellectual history in general and philosophical development in particular as we move beyond and away from the sterile oppositions of "realism" versus "idealism" (terms that characterize, between them, the Greek, Latin, and classical modern eras of philosophical history).

The major tradition of semiotic development as thus distinguished has this peculiarity, as we have seen: it includes the minor traditions but not conversely. This inclusion holds true of hermeneutics in particular (even though hermeneutics owes little or nothing to Saussure).

The reason is that hermeneutics tends to fasten onto an aspect, to a level or a phase, of the process of interpretation, namely, the linguistically specific phase, a phase that is distinctively human, but that is developed within hermeneutics in ways that tend, by overemphasizing the distinctively human possibilities, to close the distinctiveness of human interpretation in on itself in a kind of autonomous and infinite regress of semiosis. This self-enclosure of the linguistically specific phase of anthroposemiosis disguises and distorts the larger phenomenon of anthroposemiosis in its proper being as a local manifestation or region within the larger semiotic whole that must eventually be, even within interpretation, as broad as the process of semiosis in nature itself. Even that limited aspect of this process we call anthroposemiosis, in any event, assuredly includes within its compass the achievements of the natural sciences no less than those of the human sciences to which hermeneutics is over-adapted.

The semiotic point of view cannot be established theoretically by considerations that not only start from but are also confined to activities species-specifically human. Our activities of interpretation require being situated within the biological community, if we are to see with any exactitude how language emerges as something unique, that is to say, species-specific, to the population of human organisms within a larger semiosis. For this, it will also be necessary to clarify and remove definitively the all but universal confusion of language with communication. Such confusion is what led recent researchers, for example, to think they had taught language to chimpanzees. In fact their researches had merely seduced them into channeling the communications in which the animals had been engaged all along into new modalities designated by the researchers as "linguistic", but which functioned for the animals to be trained ("taught language") as nothing more than exotic communicative modalities to be mastered as a more or less necessary adaptation to environmental novelties being imposed upon them from without by their captors. (It was as if the medievals, on designating a given wall as "seen", mistook "being seen" for a property of the wall taken in its own existence. The old debates about extrinsic denomination soon precluded any fallacy so crude, but those conversations of Latin times were long forgotten by the time trainers of Sarah and Washoe applied for research grants! The animals, of course, like every other form of life, had been communicating all along, for which language remained completely unnecessary. The designation of a communicative modality as language, moreover, does not in any wise make that modality linguistic on the side of the modality used, any more than the designation of a wall as seen locates a property on the part of the wall.)

In these terms, it may be said that the semiotic standpoint results in a framework that gives a context to just the sorts of things that texts provide and that hermeneutics exegetes. This standpoint is particularly useful in showing those working in the area of literary concerns that an exclusive preoccupation with artifacts and the human activities of interpretation at that level is simply too narrow for semiotics as a whole. When such a preoccupation is taken by itself it leads to autism. Not to perceive that a maturely developed semiotic point of view provides a larger context for narrativity as something implied in, rather than defined by, the semiotic standpoint *ab initio* (as an implication of its adoption, so to say) is behind the persistent confusion (in the works of Ricoeur, for example, and in popular academic culture generally) of *semiotics* with *structuralism*. In fact, as we have already seen, structuralism, far from being the whole of semiotics, is only an aspect of semiotics. Indeed, when structuralism is pursued *as if* it were the semiotic whole, its practitioners simply import into the fresh vistas of semiotics the stale consequences of modern idealism, wherein the only thing known by the mind in all of its contexts is what the mind itself constructs.

One of the main themes and consequences of semiotics in this regard is to provide a strategy for getting beyond the terms of the debate within philosophy, literature, and history generally between realism and idealism (comparable to the terms of the debate between "capitalism" and "communism"). I have seen audiences go into mild shock over the thought that one does not have to choose between the two, but can instead simply move beyond them.

I may put this another way. An essential function of the semiotic point of view, what I think will come to be regarded as its decisive achievement historically, is its having grounded and given rise to a strategy for transcending the opposition in philosophy between the so-called realism of ancient and medieval times and the distinctively modern dilemma characterized by the label of idealism with its many forms (including "materialism", "positivism", and so forth). In other words, the requirements of semiotics cannot be met in the terms of any perspectives already established. The first requirement of semiotics is that it be developed on its own. The attempt to meet this requirement reveals from the outset that semiotics is capable of mediating a change of intellectual epoch and culture as profound and total as was the separating of medieval from ancient Greek times, or the separating of modern times from the medieval Latin era.

The reason for this is that a new definition and understanding of reality, of what we mean by "the real" as providing a focus of concern for and within human experience, is implicit in the standpoint of semiotic. Along with this new or redefinition of reality goes a dramatic paradigm shift in our notion of what is "objective" in its proper contrast with "subjective" being and "subjectivity" of every kind. Something of this has already come to light in our opening discussion. Much more will come into view in the chapters that follow, to be explained at every point in terms that have their bases in each person's own experience.

Thus I hope to show how the semiotic point of view naturally expands, given the simple realization stated above, to include the whole phenomenon of human communication—not only language—and, both after and as a consequence of that, cultural phenomena as incorporative of, as well as in their difference from, the phenomena of nature. The comprehensive integrity of this expansion is utterly dependent upon the inclusion of linguistic phenomena within the scheme of experience in a way that does not conceal or find paradoxical or embarrassing the single most decisive and striking feature of human language, which is, namely, its power to convey the nonexistent with a facility every bit equal to its power to convey thought about what is existent.

Let me make an obiter dictum on this point. When I was working at the Institute for Philosophical Research with Mortimer Adler on a book about language (i.1969–1974, a collaboration which did not work out), I was reading exclusively contemporary authors—all the logical positivist literature, the analytic philosophical literature, all of Chomsky that had been written to that date—in a word, the then-contemporary literature on language. And what I found in the central authors of the modern logico-linguistic developments—I may mention notably Frege, Wittgenstein, Russell, Carnap, Ayer, and even Brentano with regard to the use of intentionality as a tool of debate (Deely 1975, 1978)—was that they were mainly intent on finding a way to assert a one-to-one correspondence between language and mind-independent reality and to say that the only time that language is really working is when it conveys that correspondence. In fact, however, much of what we talk about and think about in everyday experience is irreducible to some kind of a prejacent physical reality in that sense. There is no atomic structure to the world such that words can be made to correspond to it point-by-point. Nor is there any structure at all to which words correspond point-by-point except the structure of discourse itself, which is hardly fixed, and which needs no such prejacent structure in order to be what it is and to signify as it does.

It is wonderful to look at the history of science and culture generally from this point of view, which is, moreover, essential for a true anthropology. The celestial spheres believed to be real for some two thousand years occupied huge treatises written to explain their functioning within the physical environment. Other examples include more simple and short-lived creatures that populate the development of the strictest science, such as phlogiston, the ether, the planet Vulcan; and examples can be multiplied from every sphere. The complete history of human discourse, including the hard sciences, is woven around unrealities that functioned once as real in the thinking and theorizing and experience of some peoples. The planet Vulcan (my own favorite example alongside the canals of Mars) thus briefly but embarrassingly turned up as interior to the orbit of Mercury in some astronomy work at the turn of the last century. But Vulcan then proved not to exist outside those reports at all. The objective notion of ether played a long and distinguished role in post-Newtonian physical science—as central in its own way as the celestial spheres were in the Ptolemaic phase of astronomy's development—before proving similarly to be a chimera.

So the problem of how we talk about nonexistent things, where nonexistent means nonexistent in the physical sense, is a fundamental positive problem with which the whole movement of so-called linguistic philosophy fails to come to terms. This is not just a matter of confusion, nor just a matter of language gone on holiday, but of the essence, as we will see, of human language.

To understand this fundamental insouciance of language, whereby it imports literary elements of nonbeing and fictional characters even into the sternest science and most realistic concerns of philosophy, we will find it necessary to reinterpret language from the semiotic point of view. For this, it is not enough to recognize that language itself is a system of relationships and contrasts between elements. We shall see that language itself as an objective network is part of a larger whole of objective relations, what I will call in chapter 5 the Umwelt or "objective world" of experience integrally taken, in relation to which the linguistic network exists symbiotically—that is, as itself feeding upon and being transformed by the structure of experience as a whole in its irreducibility to the physical environment. In a word, it will be necessary to see how language is a form, but only a form, of semiosis and of semiosis only in its anthroposemiotic modality.

I will proceed as follows. First I will outline in chapter 3 the basic subject matter of semiotic inquiry, which is the activity proper to signs, or semiosis. This, indeed, will establish the outline for the book as a whole, indicating at the same time the scope of the perspective properly called semiotic and the myriad of methods—both traditional and not yet developed—necessary to mine this perspective in full. Then in chapter 4 I will investigate what it is about the sign that makes it capable of acting or functioning in the manner peculiar to it.

From these general considerations providing the outlines of semiotics in its prospective totality, I will move in chapter 5 to the specific consideration of the action of signs within our experience, because it is best to establish the basic notions as the elements of a science cenoscopically considered, that is to say, in terms that are derived from what is accessible to everyone, namely, common experience. At the same time, we will see that what gives experience its irreducible quality is something quite different from what makes experience specifically human. In this way, still proceeding cenoscopically, we will be able to reach, from within anthroposemiosis, by purely analytical means, the central concept of zoösemiosis as well,[5] the

---

5. The relation between anthroposemiosis and zoösemiosis thus is an intimate one. In the evolution of life, the human Umwelt, or Lebenswelt, developed out of, and as a species-specifically unique variation on, an Umwelt or structure of experience common more or less to any anthropoid and, in differing ways, to all animal forms. Nonetheless, not only because our concern here is with the basic concepts considered in a cenoscopic way, but also for the reason stated by von Uexküll (1934, 48: "the real problem, in all its implications, can only be analyzed in man"), it will be necessary for us to proceed the other way around. We will derive the basic notions of objective world from the side of human experience. These in hand, we are then in a position to construct the Umwelt of zoösemiosis analytically by subtracting the species-specific experience of stipulatability from the structure of human experience, and taking the remainder in its possible being as further specifiable—that is, able to be determined in this or that way—according as it is subsumed under this or that organismic structure within biology, such as idioscopic research shows to be required in each specific case.

The required procedure here has no generally recognized name in philosophical tradition, as far as I know. The basic procedure, as far removed from anthropomorphism as possible, nonetheless depends expressly on avoiding the mistake of behaviorism in American psy-

Umwelt or "objective world", inasmuch as the structure of human experience in its fundamental objectivity, though not in all of its specificity, is the common structure and factor in the experience as such of any animal.[6]

The newly opened panorama of semiosis at the plant level, both within and beyond the human environment as such, is as intriguing a concept as it is controversial, well deserving a serious reflection upon its place within the developing scheme of semiotics as a whole. No less intriguing—though even less well established—is the question of the distinctive causality of semiosis as it operates or might be operative in the physical universe at those levels—both microscopic and macroscopic—and in those spheres quite independent of plant life (as the animal and human zones of semiosis emphatically are not). Thus, in order to situate fully phytosemiosis in its prejacency to zoösemiosis and anthroposemiosis, it will be necessary to try in chapter 6 to give some body to the highly abstract but central notion of "objective" or "extrinsic formal" causality–the causality that makes the action of signs *sui generis* and almost equally at home among existent and nonexistent actors of the here and now—as it applies also to the universe at large on the environmental side of the interaction of bodies.

With this our outline of the subject matter as a whole will be completed. We will have proceeded, in the main, synchronically, with no more than a few diachronic allusions. The allusions need to be drawn together, and this is the task of chapter 7. The whole at this point will have made

---

chology. The biological inheritance of the human observer must itself be accounted for in the observer–observed equation as an interpretant in the semiosis. It is a question of recognizing the difference between naive and participant observation (T. von Uexküll 1982; Williams 1982).

I was first made aware of the requirements of the problem as an undergraduate, in a more obscure form and under a more unlikely label. My then-professor Ralph Austin Powell used to insist that a correct reading of the *De Anima* of Aristotle required interpreting the living world by way of what he called *humanesque analogy*, that is to say, by an analytical comparison from within our own experience of being alive. The term never caught on, and, as far as I know, Powell gradually abandoned the effort to make it clear in the abstract context of his philosophical conceptions.

Had Powell been a more empirically minded thinker, and familiar in particular with the work of J. von Uexküll, he would have found needed exemplifications readier to hand for effectively communicating the nature of the so-called "humanesque analogy".

Sebeok (1989b: 81), himself a student of J. von Uexküll in this regard, summarizes the semiotic dimension of the observer–observed problem, where the observer is of the human species and the observed is of another grouping of life rather than a conspecific: "what may constitute a 'sign' in the Umwelt of the observed organism is inaccessible to the observer. The solution to this seemingly intractable dilemma, according to J. von Uexküll, presupposes that the would-be observer of the behavior of another organism begin by analyzing her own Umwelt before she can undertake productive observations of the behavior of speechless creatures. It is by way of such a comparative analysis that we are led back straight into the heart of semiosis in our human world."

Hence, we combine our initial treatment of zoösemiosis with that of anthroposemiosis and, subsequently, of physiosemiosis with phytosemiosis. The latter two, for all their differences, have in common that they are the levels at which the possibility of an objective world is rendered actual; whereas the former two, for all their differences, have in common that unmistakable something that is consequent upon the semiotic point of view, if not always unmistakably so, namely, the centrality of history as the anthroposemiotic transmission of culture to the doctrine of signs and to the proper life of human understanding even in its most "scientific" moments and synchronically conceived investigations. Thus, with the basic concepts synchronically and prospectively established, it will be time to close with some retrospective considerations, providing at least briefly and by way of an outline some remarks on the history of semiotics itself, as its shape has begun to form in the mists of the past, from the standpoint of its basic concepts and the "theory" of semiotics.

So the outline for the remaining chapters is as follows: semiosis, signs, zoö- and anthroposemiotics, phyto- and physiosemiotics, and the theory and historical outline of semiotics itself as a distinctive form of human consciousness. Such I deem to be the basics of semiotics, because these subject-areas or themes taken in concert show what is interesting and possible for semiotics as a phenomenon of intellectual culture. These are the concepts that establish the full amplitude of the semiotic point of view and reveal on the basis of that viewpoint the indefinite methodological possibilities for enriching in detail our understanding of a phenomenon as unified and yet as diverse as the action of signs, whereby indeed we exist in community and wherein the mind finds its proper food for thought.

---

they are the levels at which objective worlds in their irreducible "reality" are constituted and diversified.
6. Thus, it is a matter of semiotics idioscopically pursued—pursued, that is to say, with all the panoply of special investigations and instruments science brings to bear—to say with regard to any given animal species, especially the more removed the forms are from the human (such as mollusks, balloon flies, etc.), how this common structure is actually determined and enhanced or diminished in the multiply species-specific patterns or ways of life actually found in the environment.

3

SEMIOSIS: THE SUBJECT MATTER
OF SEMIOTIC INQUIRY

IF WE ASK what it is that semiotic studies investigate, the answer is, in a word, action. The action of signs.

This peculiar type of action, corresponding to the distinctive type of knowledge that the name semiotic properly characterizes, has long been recognized in philosophy in connection with investigations of the various types of physical causality. But in that connection, the "ideal" or objective factor, the pattern according to which the investigations themselves were able to establish the material, formal, and determinative dimensions of causality in the productive or "efficient" sense, appeared as something marginal. This objective factor pertains more to the observation than to the observed in its independent existence. Hence this factor was not clearly pertinent to the results of investigations which did not have as their aim the establishment of any essential connection as such between observer and observed, such as would make "observation"—an extrinsic formal connection between subject knowing and subject known—even possible in the first place.

Some of the most difficult and extended passages in Poinsot's early attempt (1632a) to systematize the foundations of semiotic inquiry arise from the need to make this heretofore peripheral topic of natural inquiry central to the establishment of semiotic (see, for example, Questions 2–5 in Book I of his *Treatise on Signs*). More recently, in this same context of inquiry, Ralph Powell (1986, 1988) has managed to indicate how central this neglected and previously obscure type of causality is to the whole problematic of epistemology, once its semiotic character has been recognized.

Not until about 1906, however, was the peculiar action of signs singled out as a distinct field of possible inquiry in its own right, rather than through its adjacency with other lines of immediate investigation, and given a proper name. The investigator who singled out this field by giving it a name of its own was Charles Sanders Peirce, and the name he assigned to it was *semiosis*. At this point the doctrine of signs turned a corner in its development: Peirce saw that the full development of semiotic as a distinct body of knowledge required a dynamic view of signification as a process. Semiotics could not be merely a response to the question of the being proper to signs ontologically considered. Response must also be made to the further question of the becoming this peculiar type of being enables and sustains itself by. Symbols do not just exist; they also grow.

Semiosis as a type of activity is distinctive in that it always involves three elements, but it is even more distinctive in that one of these three elements need not be an actual existent thing. In all other types of action, the actors are correlative, and, hence, the action between them, however many there may be, is essentially dyadic and dynamical. For it to occur, both terms must exist. A car cannot hit a tree unless the tree is there to. be hit, but a sign can signify an upcoming bridge that is no longer there. Galileo's eyes and telescope engaged in a dynamic interaction with light from the stars. But over and above this dynamic interaction he essayed opinions concerning the celestial spheres that turned out not to exist. And yet the nonbeing of these spheres contributed to Galileo's imprisonment and propositions concerning them were cited as grounds for the serious sanctions taken against Galileo by the authorities.

Peirce calls the action as such between existent things "brute force" or "dynamical interaction". It may be physical, or it may be psychological. In either case, the action takes place between two subjects of physical existence and is, in a terminology we shall be obliged to both clarify and insist upon along our way, always and irreducibly a *subjective interaction*. Subjective interactions, whether psychical or physical, are always involved in the action of signs, but they surround the semiosis as its context and condition, while always falling short of the action of signs proper. In other words, while the action of signs always involves dynamical interactions, dynamical interactions need not always involve the action of signs.

The distinctiveness of semiosis is unavoidable when we consider the case of two existing things affected in the course of their existence by what does not exist, but, if we understand what is distinctive about semiosis, that distinctiveness remains unmistakable even when the three terms involved in a semeiosy happen also to be all three existent. Peirce gives the example of the rise of the mercury in a thermometer, which is brought about "in a purely brute and dyadic way" by the increase of ambient warmth, but which, on being perceived by someone familiar with thermometers, also produces the idea of increasing warmth in the environment. This idea as a mental event belongs entirely to the order of subjective and physical existence, no more and no less than does the rising mercury and the ambient temperature of the thermometer's environs. It is, as Peirce puts it, the "immediate object" of the thermometer taken as a certain type of sign, namely, one indexical of an environmental condition.

The object of the thermometer as a sign is the relative warmth of the surroundings. The object of the idea of the thermometer as a sign is no different. The thermometer, however, prior to being read is involved only in dynamical interactions. On being read a third factor enters in, the factor of interpretation. The thermometer on being seen may not be recognized as a thermometer: in that case, besides being a subject of physical interactions, that is to say, a thing, it becomes also a cognized or known thing, an element of experience or object. But, if it is both seen and recognized as a thermometer, it is not only a thing become object but also an object become sign. As a thing it merely exists, a node of sustenance for a network of physical relations and actions. As an object it also exists for someone as an element of experience, differentiating a perceptual field in definite ways related to its being as a thing among other elements of the environment. But as a sign it stands not only for itself within experience and in the environment but also for something else as well, something besides itself. It not only exists (thing), it not only stands to someone (object), it also stands to someone for something else (sign). And this "something else" may or may not be real in the physical sense: what it indicates may be misleading, if, for example, the thermometer is defective.

In this case, its immediate object, the idea it produces as sign, becomes in its turn a node of sustenance for a network of relations presumed to be physical but that in fact, because of the defective nature of the thermometer being observed, is merely objective. Here we encounter a primary phenomenon that semiotic analysis is obliged to take into account: divisions of things as things and divisions of objects as objects are not the same and vary independently, the former being determined directly by physical action alone, the latter being mediated indirectly by semeiosy, the action of signs.[7]

The immediate point to be noted is this: Divisions of objects as objects and divisions of things as things may happen to coincide, as when the thermometer seen and recognized is also functioning properly; or they

---

7. The contrast between objective being and the subjective order of physical existence was noted early in the development of an explicitly semiotic consciousness, for example, in the work of Cajetan (1507). But its centrality to the doctrine of signs only gradually came into view. Like the geological fault presaging major changes in the lay of the land, the inherent difference between objective and physical existence at the heart of being made it inevitable that dynamical interactions, overall, would give rise to directional changes, and with them to transformations of crude atomic structures to the point where semiotic animals would wander where once cosmic dust and random interactions obtained. But this takes us too far from the simplicity of our example and the fundamental point it makes for the doctrine of signs.

may happen to diverge, as when the thermometer seen and recognized is, unbeknownst to its interpreter, deceptive by defect. But, even when they coincide, the two orders remain irreducible in what is proper to them.[8]

The idea of surrounding temperature produced by the thermometer as sign represents to the interpreter of the thermometer something that itself is neither the idea nor the thermometer, namely, the presumed condition of the environment indexically represented by the thermometer. The idea as a mental representation, that is to say, a psychological reality, belongs to the order of subjective existence and is the immediate object of the thermometer as sign. But, within that order, the idea also functions to found a relation to something other than itself, namely, a condition of the environment surrounding the thermometer, which condition is both objective (known) and physical (something existent besides being known), presuming the thermometer accurate; or merely objective but deviant from the physical situation rather than coincident with it, presuming the thermometer defective. As founding this relation, in every case objective, in some cases coincidentally physical as well, the idea itself produced by the thermometer has in turn produced "the proper significate outcome" of the thermometer as sign. This Peirce calls the *interpretant*, a unique and important notion, the key to understanding the action of signs as a process, a form of becoming, as well as a kind of being, over and above the unique essential structure that makes signification possible in the first place.

---

8. It is for this reason that I have resisted the temptation of tying the basic categorial concepts and terminology of biosemiosis to the latest biological theories which have, for solid reasons (e.g., see Sagan and Margulis 1987, Margulis and Sagan 1986, 1986a), replaced the traditional two kingdoms with five (not unlike the manner in which the traditional five external senses provide a cenoscopic framework of discussion for psychology within which idioscopic research is able to demonstrate that there are actually more refined discriminations which validate recognition of a greater number of sensory channels). At the same time, the intrinsically semiotic character of the new divisions, resting as they do on the introduction of symbiosis and reciprocity into the heart of the evolutionary process along with the selection of mutations, makes of these new concepts an extremely fertile ground for the further development of semiotic consciousness, and an inevitable frontier that semiotic theory cannot for long delay exploring.

Nonetheless, because these results are idioscopic rather than cenoscopic (as Sagan and Margulis 1987 put it, "Although many plant and animal symbionts are known, symbiosis and its fundamental role in evolution really become conspicuous in the microcosm"), and because the divisions of semiosis pertain to the objective order directly and to the physical order indirectly (the very opposite of the divisions of organismic types traditionally sought by biology as a natural science), a detailed attempt to incorporate these theories seemed to me premature for the project of the present work. As we noted in our collaborative "manifesto" of 1984 (Anderson, Deely, Ransdell, Sebeok, T. von Uexküll: 42–43), even though, "with the five-kingdom classification, 'plants' and 'animals' return through the looking glass to become strictly folk taxa once more", it does not follow that what is called for is to "simply reparcel semiosis according to the putative five kingdoms, not only because these are provisional, as we noted above, and will doubtless remain so for some time, but because, more fundamentally, they may not even be interesting or significant in sorting out different *types* of semiosis".

From the point of view of basic semiotics as something to be achieved first cenoscopically and established as equally important for the understanding of the *literati* and the *scientisti*, what is essential is first to grasp macroscopically the difference cognition makes within the

Peirce suggests (c.1906: 5.473) that "it is very easy to see what the interpretant of a sign is: it is all that is explicit in the sign itself apart from its context and circumstances of utterance". In the case at hand: the sign is the thermometer; the context and circumstances of its utterance are the ambient warmth producing a certain level of the mercury correlated— accurately or inaccurately, as we have seen—with a scale, the whole of which apparatus is seen and recognized as a temperature measuring device; and what is explicit in the sign itself apart from this context and these circumstances is representation of something other than the thermometer, namely, the ambient temperature, as being presumably at what the thermometer indicates it to be, although this may be wrong due to defect in the mechanism. In other words, all that is explicit in the sign itself apart from its context and circumstances of utterance is "its proper significate outcome", the objective element of the situation as involving representation of one by another, irreducible to the dynamical interactions involved, and establishing channels and expectations along which some of the interactions will be diverted in ongoing exchanges.

In our example, the idea of the thermometer enabling the thermometer to function as a sign was in the first instance a mental representation. The interpretant of a sign, however—and this is a very important point— "need not be a mental mode of being", nor, as we have seen, is it as mental mode of being that the idea produced by the thermometer functions as interpretant. Whether a given interpretant be an idea or not, what is essential to it as interpretant is that it be the ground upon which the sign is seen to be related to something else as signified, which signified in turn be-

---

order of living things, and, within cognition, the proper role of language within experience of the universe with its natural, social, and cultural elements as these bear on "the difference between a naive and a participant observer".

The realization that the latter is not so much, as Thure von Uexküll puts it (1982: 12), a "choice" as it is the actual situation of our species (within which the illusion of the naive observer arises) is what a grasp of semiotic fundamentals makes unavoidable. This realization, as he well says (ibid.), "will determine our understanding of animals, plants, and human beings", along with the physical surroundings of life, all the way to the stars.

Within this basic perspective, not only is there all the room in the world for the further refinements and adjustments of idioscopy of whatever kind, but such refinements and adjustments become inevitable, beginning with the redistribution of biological life forms according to new requirements and discoveries of research which bring out, in the manner of the new views in biology, the essentially semiotic character of the organismic development of all the plants and animals. It is not only the "self", as Sebeok has pointed out, that is a semiotic phenomenon: the "other" is no less semiotic, making of the biosphere in its totality "a flowing pointillist landscape where each dot of paint is also alive" (Sagan and Margulis 1987: 33).

Thus, the temporary bypassing of detailed discussion of the latest perspectives in evolutionary biology here is tactical, not strategic. Far from obviating the need to integrate the sciences no less than the humanities into the theoretical texture of semiotic development, the present work intends to make that need all the more evident and pressing, as chapter 6 in particular will show. (And it hardly bears reminding that, in modern times, the stance of the naive observer and the population of scientists have tended to be roughly coextensive or, in linguistic terms, synonyms.)

comes a sign relative to other elements in the experience of the interpreter, setting in motion the chain of interpretants on which semiosis as a process feeds. In other words, what is essential to the interpretant is that it mediate the difference between objective and physical being, a difference that knows no fixed line. This is the reason why, at the same time, the triadic production of the interpretant is essential to a sign, and the interpretant need not be a mental mode of being, although, considered as founding a determinate relation of signification for some animal, it will be.

We see now with greater clarity the difference between the action of signs and the action of things. The action of signs is purely objective, always at once involving and exceeding the action of things as such, while the action of things as such is purely subjective or, what comes to the same thing, physical or psychic and restricted to the order of what exists here and now.[9]

Wherever the future influences a present course of events, therefore, we are confronted by semiosis. Never confined to what has been or is, semiosis transpires at the boundary between what is and what might be or might have been. Linguistic signs may well be "the ideological phenomenon par excellence", as Vološinov said (1929: 13); but the action of signs, which provides the general subject matter of semiotic inquiry, extends well beyond what we call "language", even though it is only through language that this range can be brought to light for us as inquirers. Why this is so we shall eventually see.

In order to appreciate the privileged and at the same time restricted role of linguistic signs in semiosis, however, it is necessary to get these peculiar signs into a larger perspective revealing something of the other processes, no less semiosic, on which the possibility and actuality of linguistic semioses depend. For this purpose, it is useful to outline in broad terms a number of levels within semiosis. These levels, of course, can be further distinguished indefinitely for purposes of specialized research and investigation. Here it will be enough to bring out in a synoptic way the prospective scope of semiotic inquiry, an effort that should also have the effect of neutralizing the vestigial inclinations to positivism and modern idealism that often in practice corrupt the semiotic standpoint by assimilat-

---

9. Peirce's way of putting this is obscure, outside the framework of his technical semiotic: thirdness, he says, always presupposes the brute interactions of secondness which also always presupposes the dream world which secondness differentiates, firstness. Thus, on the basis of his "recognition of ten respects in which Signs may be divided", Peirce concludes (1908b: 8.343; see also 1904) that "since every one of them turns out to be a trichotomy, it follows that in order to decide what classes of signs result from them, I have 3^{10}, or 59049, difficult questions to carefully consider". For present purposes, and following the example of Peirce himself at this point (who did "not undertake to carry [his] systematical division of signs any further", but left that "for future explorers"), clarification of this technical way of phrasing the situation may safely be left to the exegetes of the Peircean texts. The aim here is to reach a more general audience.

ing it to what is irretrievably presemiotic in the previous era and most recent epoch of philosophy.

The highest level of semiosis so far as our experience goes is also the one closest to us: *anthroposemiosis*. Looked at one way, anthroposemiosis includes all of the sign processes that human beings are directly involved in, and, looked at another way, names those sign processes which are species-specifically human. From the latter point of view, anthroposemiosis includes first of all language, and secondly those sign systems that come after language and further structure perception and modify the environment even for species of animals other than human, although the understanding of these postlinguistic changes in what is proper to them is possible only in and through language.

For this reason, language has come to be called in Eastern European circles of semiotic development the "primary modeling system" and the rest of human culture and civilization a series of "secondary modeling systems". As Sebeok in particular has taken pains to point out (1987), however, this way of describing the situation is not entirely satisfactory, because it is grounded, as is apparent, in a derivative understanding of anthroposemiosis. More fundamentally and inclusively, anthroposemiosis comprises, as we have said, all of the sign processes that human beings are directly involved in. From this point of view, language itself is already a secondary modeling system, not the primary one, even though, relative to the distinctively human cultural traditions and developments of civilization, language is the proximate enabling medium and sustaining network of semiosis. Proximate to language, however, is the larger semiotic web of human experience that intricately interweaves linguistic semiosis with perceptual semioses shared in common with other biological species. This larger web delicately depends upon endosemiotic networks within the body whereby the human organism itself is sustained by a complex network of symbioses without which the human individual would perish, and which network proves in its own right to be a thoroughly semiosic one.

In addition, the interaction between human being and physical environment—whereby, for example, a person noting the sky anticipates stormy weather and prepares accordingly—gives rise to further strands of the semiotic web linking the human being not only with conspecifics and not only with other animals, but also with the general realm of physical surroundings in the largest sense. From this point of view, anthroposemiosis forms a seamless whole with all of nature, and the appropriate metaphor is not that of language as a primary modeling system but the ancient one of *anthropos* as *microcosmos*. Anthroposemiosis is the most complex form of semiosis not because it harbors unique modes of semiosis, beginning with language, but because, in addition to harboring unique developments, it harbors at the same time all the other semiosic developments as well and depends upon them in achieving whatever is unique and specific to itself, beginning with language.

The semiosic processes of perception and sensation that are common to other animals besides the human define the level and zone of what Sebeok and Wells first characterized as *zoösemiosis* (Sebeok 1963: 74). To their original coinage I add the umlaut, to prevent a misunderstanding that I have actually encountered, whereby this rich realm has been unwittingly reduced in hearers' minds to the study of sign systems among captive animals.

Like anthroposemiosis, zoösemiosis can be regarded from two standpoints. From one point of view, zoösemiosis is concerned with the overlap of semiotic processes shared between human animals and other animal forms. But this point of view provides only part of the story, for each animal species, not only the human one, develops also species-specific semiotic modalities, and these too are the province of zoösemiotic investigations. The splendid work of von Frisch (1950) unraveling the species-specific semiosis of bees, or of Kessel (1955) in uncovering the species-specific symbolic component in mating activities of balloon flies, provide landmark examples of zoösemiotic analysis beyond the study of semiotic systems shared between human and other animals (although humans do indeed mate and benefit, too, from the dance of bees). From the point of view of zoösemiosis as concerned with the study of species-specific semiotic modalities developed among the biological forms other than human, we can see an entire regrouping of naturalist studies (which have their own distinguished traditions) under a new label more appropriate to and specificative of what naturalists have been trying to accomplish all along. Like anthroposemiosis, zoösemiosis comprises a series of microcosms and species-specific objective worlds as well, each one entangled in natural processes of physical interaction (secondness) as well as in semiosic processes of objective interaction within and across species. The collective whole forms an interlocking network of irreducibly semiotic relations, many of which are physical as well as objective, many of which are purely objective in specifically diverse patterns.

Most recently, a third macroscopic realm and level of semiosis within nature has been surveyed and established, under the rubric of *phytosemiosis*, the semiotic networks of plants, by the distinguished work of Martin Krampen and his coworkers. Here again a twofold standpoint is possible. There is undoubtedly semiosic interaction between plants and various species of animals, as the many insect victims of plants such as the notorious "venus fly-trap" mutely testify. It is surely remarkable, for example, that many plants grow in a form that is sexually deceiving to species of insect on which the propagation or nutrition of the plant depends. The plant world is replete with these astonishing examples of the extrinsic formal causality at the heart of sign activity. But there is also the question of semiosis within the plant world itself, as the recent discovery that trees are able to inform one another of zones of infection, for example, raises.

Here we reach a boundary line, which we may nonetheless cross by means of abduction, that is, the formulation of some hypothesis suggesting new ideas for the further extension of the boundaries of semiotic activity to include the realm of so-called inorganic nature, both chemical and physical. These ideas need to be developed, tested, and further refined or even rejected by whole teams of workers.

Besides the three main levels of semiosis that have been briefly described above and are firmly established regions of sign activity, there is reason to think that sign activity has also been at work in an anticipatory way even at inorganic levels before the advent of life in nature, as is suggested by the formula established by Poinsot (1632a: 126/3–4): "it suffices to be a sign virtually in order to signify in act". This formula derives from carefully considering the fact that all that pertains to secondness and dyadic interaction in semiosis belongs to signs strictly through what in them provides the foundations or fundaments whence result or might result relations of representation of another in which signifying consists formally as thirdness.[10] Sign activity in the inorganic realm would, according to this formula, occur less visibly and in the background, then, but virtually and as a matter of fact throughout the material realm.

On this hypothesis, there is not only the macroscopic realm of *biosemiosis* whose three main levels have been outlined and named, with plenty of indication of microscopic subcurrents equally semiosic, as in the case of endosemiosis stated by Sebeok. There is also the more inclusive macroscopic realm of evolution in general, let us call it *physiosemiosis*, an activity virtual by comparison with biosemiosis but no less replete with the objective causality whereby the physical interaction of existing things is channeled toward a future different from what obtains at the time of the affected interaction. This is a process whereby first stars and then planetary systems develop out of a more primitive atomic and molecular "dust", but these systems in turn give rise to conditions under which further complexifications of atomic structure become possible. Some of these possibilities, inevitably, become actual as well (such as an oxidizing atmosphere, to choose a local example), continuing the process, as I have shown elsewhere (1969: shown, that is, as definitively as anything can be shown in the absence of directly observed data), along an overall trajectory inevitably pointing to the establishment of biosemiosic phenomena.

---

10. In current parlance, it is the vehicle of the sign, rather than the sign itself formally, that, for example, can be washed away in a flood, fall over on something passing by, or, at another leave, "produce a sense impression", and so forth.

On this hypothesis, semiosis, as providing the subject matter of semiotic investigation, would establish nothing less than a new framework and foundation for the whole of human knowledge. This new framework and foundation would embrace not only the so-called human and social sciences, as we have already seen from the partial tradition of semiology after Saussure, but also the so-called "hard" or natural sciences, precisely as they, too, arise from within and depend in their development upon experience and the processes of anthroposemiosis generally, as the wholistic tradition of semiotics after Peirce has begun to outline.

In many basic respects this is a contemporary development, but it draws its nourishment from long ago and has its own distinguished lineage of pioneers and precursors. In particular, we see here a contemporary development fulfilling the prophecy of Winance (1983: 515): "It is in the tradition of Peirce, Locke, and Poinsot that Logic becomes Semiotic, able to assimilate the whole of epistemology and natural philosophy as well". In Winance's remark, "epistemology" is to be taken as a synecdoche for the human sciences, and "natural philosophy" as a synecdoche for the natural sciences including, as Aquinas noted (c.1269: Book I, lectio 1, n. 2), "even metaphysics". Representing our answer to the question of what semiotics investigates integrally, that is, including in a single scheme both what is firmly established and what we abductively extrapolated, we may outline the overall subject matter of semiotic investigations as in Figure 1.

Regardless of our hypothetical extension of semiosis beyond the boundaries of the biological community—whether, that is, we wish to stick with the firmly established levels or wish also to consider the possibilities of a physiosemiosis in nature antecedent to and subtensive of the later and more restricted phenomena of biosemiosis—what is clear at this point is that semiotics is the name for a distinctive series of investigations, distinctive for the same reason that any investigation is distinctive, namely, by reason of what it studies, in the present case, semiosis. But how is such an activity as semiosis possible in the first place?

through the development
of semiotic modalities
between other animals and
humans, of language within
the human species, and
consequently of historical
traditions and culture
generally: ANTHROPOSEMIOSIS ⌐

through the development   in the organic
of semiotic modalities   realm as such
between plants and animals,   (as including
among animals, and between   endosemiotic
animals and the physical   processes):
surroundings: ZOÖSEMIOSIS ──────┼── BIOSEMIOSIS ──────┐

through the development   the action
of semiotic modalities   of signs
within the plant kingdom   or
and between plants and   ⌐ SEMIOSIS
the physical surroundings:
PHYTOSEMIOSIS ──────────┘

through the initial
condensation of   in the physical
stellar systems ────────────┐   environment
                            │   as such:
through the subsequent   ├───────── PHYSIOSEMIOSIS ─┘
development of planetary   │
and subplanetary systems ───┘

FIGURE 1.   *The Levels of Semiosis* (columns of table read from left
            to right)

SIGNS:
THE MEDIUM OF SEMIOSIS

MOTION IS THE act of the agent in the patient: so goes the classic definition of dynamic action or "brute force", what the scholastics called "transitive action", that is, action that passes from one thing to another through the production of change. In Aristotle's categories of physical being, action and passion (punching and being punched, say) are dyadic, strictly correlative, the one as initiating and the other as terminating. The resultant change is the action of the agent transpiring in the patient, that is, in the one undergoing the action, and its traces endure as part of the physical order itself (principally in the patient as outcome but in the agent, too, as vestiges and clues).

The action of signs is entirely different. It is not productive of change directly. It is always mediated. It lacks the directness of punching and being punched. Even when the semiosis is involved with dyadic dynamicity, as it always is, though to varying degrees, what gives the action of signs its curiously detached and ethereal quality is precisely its indirection, what Peirce rightly characterized as its irreducible *triadicity*. The sign not only stands for something other than itself, it does so for some third; and though these two relations—sign to signified, sign to interpretant— may be taken separately, when they are so taken, there is no longer a question of sign but of cause to effect on one hand and object to knowing subject on the other. In short, for the relation of sign to signified to exist in its proper being as semiotic (smoke as a sign of fire, let us say), regardless of whether that relation exists dyadically as well (say, as an effect to cause relation between smoke and something burning), reference to the future in a third element, the interpretant, is essential. And this third element is essential, regardless of whether the thirdness is actual here and now or only virtual and "waiting to be realized" (as in a bone to be discovered next year as having belonged to an extinct species of dinosaur not previously known to have wandered as far as Montana).

Seeing that the being proper to signs has, historically, this essentially and irreducible triadic character was an insight hard come by, as Poinsot's survey of the opinions contesting as late as 1632 attests (*Tractatus de Signis*, Book I, Question 2, esp. 154/35ff.). In certain respects, the point did not become fully centralized thematically within the doctrine of signs until Peirce displaced the ontological typologies of earlier semiotic analyses with the epigenetic typologies of the sign considered as the nexus and but temporarily "fixed foot" in a continuing and continuous process of signification, wherein the relation between objective and physical being constitutive of experience and modificative of each physical *status quo* is sustained dynamically (and hence dependent throughout). Nonetheless, the essential point was established early that (Poinsot 1632a: 157/38–41) "in the very innards and intimate rationale of such a substitution for and representation of a signified", as is a sign, there is an indirection over and above any directly physical connection. Peirce's later work serves to underscore that the original controversies had resulted in a definitive achievement of semiotic analysis, which Poinsot formulated thus (1632a: 156/23–157/10, 157/19–27):

> Although an object in respect of a power is not constituted essentially in a relation to that power, but rather does the power depend upon the object, nevertheless, in the case of a sign, which is vicegerent for an object in the representing and exhibiting of itself to a power, this relation is necessarily included, and by a twofold necessity: both because a substitution for anything is always in an order to something, and since a sign substitutes for and functions in the capacity of the thing signified in an order to the office of representing to a power, the sign must necessarily express an order to a power; and because to represent is to make an object present to a power, therefore, if a sign is a medium and substitute of the signified in representing, it necessarily involves an order to that to which it represents or makes present.
>
> For in the case of these relations which exist in the mode of substituting and representing, it is impossible that they should respect that whose vicegerent they are, and not that on account of which or in an order to which they substitute, because it is in substituting or functioning in the capacity of another according to some determinate rationale and in an order to some determinate end that one thing is a vicegerent of that other.

It is as a result of this indirection, of their triadicity, as Peirce points out (c.1906: 5.473), that there is nothing automatic about the action of signs. The action of signs, in other words, depends upon that very feature whereby being a sign is a singularly unstable condition, and our concern here is to give an account of the uniqueness of this singularity.

The sign first of all depends on something other than itself. It is representative but only in a derivative way, in a subordinate capacity. The moment a sign slips out from under this subordination, as frequently happens, at just that moment does it cease for a while to be a sign. A sign seen standing on its own is not seen as a sign, even though it may remain one virtually.[11] Thus on its own, it is a mere object or thing become object, waiting to become a sign, perhaps, or having formerly been a sign, perhaps, but, on its own, not actually a sign at all.

So a sign is a representative, but not every representative is a sign. Things can represent themselves within experience. To the extent that they do so, they are objects and nothing more, even though in their becoming objects signs and semiosis are already invisibly at work. To be a sign, it is necessary to represent something other than the self. Being a sign is a form of bondage to another, to the signified, the object that the sign is not but that the sign nevertheless stands for and represents.

This is the most important fact about the sign, because it is what is most decisive for it: its thorough relativity. There are signs that are also objects in their own right, just as there are objects that are also things. But there are no signs that are not relative to some object other than themselves, and that object or those objects to which the sign is relative we call the signified or significate, the essential content of the sign insofar as it is a sign.

Because the essential content or being of the sign is relative, the key to understanding what is proper to the sign is the notion of relativity, relation, or relative being. Without this content, the sign ceases to be a sign, whatever else it may happen to be. Stripped of its thirdness, the sign slips back into the dyadic order of mere actual existence or, perhaps even further, into the monadic order of mere possibilities and dreams beyond which there is nowhere to go. Conversely, what enables some mere possibility or some actual physical entity to become also a sign is the fact, contingent or necessary as the case may be, that it acquires a relation to something else such that it stands for that other. So, if we can understand what it means to say that a being is a relative being, we will be in a fair position to say further what a sign is in its proper being, since this being is perforce relative. And, as we shall see, it is the peculiar and unique character of relative being—in the sense that pertains to the sign in its proper being,

---

11. That is to say again, as was mentioned in the previous chapter, that all in the sign pertaining to secondness and dyadic interaction pertains to the sign by reason of its foundation or fundament whence the sign relation arises or might arise. The sign-vehicle, rather than the sign itself formally, is what, for example, "produces a sense impression", or falls over on a passing car, or is hit by a bullet, etc.

but that also obtains physically in the order of nature independently of being experienced—that explains why such a peculiar activity as semiosis and such a peculiar phenomenon as truth and falsehood (which is an off-shoot of semiosis) is possible in the first place.

Here again we deal with a matter that has a lengthy and tangled history. As our concern is doctrinal, however, I do not have to presume intimate knowledge of the history of the question of relative being on the part of the reader. It will be enough for the present if the reader understand the terms and distinctions that will be here directly made. Then, later, he or she may investigate the historical materials that made the terms and distinctions of the present explanation possible, in order to evaluate what other reading of the historical development might also be possible and useful for advancing the understanding of semiosis.

I will proceed, therefore, to merely state the matter directly, without burdening the reader with detailed citations from and references to the many authors since Aristotle who contributed to the development of the matter to the point where a direct statement of the present sort became possible. I will instead cite only a few texts clarifying the most central points, and only from those authors, particularly Poinsot, who were able to point out directly how these central points contribute directly to establishing the basics of a doctrine of signs.

And further to ease the reader's grasp of the basic notions, let me frame the discussion of relative being with a very concrete example, put in the form of a question: When a child dies, in what sense is the child's parent a parent? The concreteness of the question may serve as an antidote to the inevitable and perhaps extreme abstractness of the subject to be explained. For in dealing with the question of relative being, particularly in that aspect decisive for understanding the activity and being proper to signs, even though we are dealing with what is most basic to the experience of all of us in its being as experience, we are yet dealing with that one aspect of direct experience which escapes entirely direct sensory perception. For relative being in this sense—the intersubjective as such—is indirectly given even at the level of sensation rationally distinguished from and within perceptions. A lover may not be understood but can at least be seen and touched. A relation in the sense constitutive of the sign in the being proper to it as sign can not be seen or touched. It can be understood, but, without that understanding, it cannot be grasped directly at all. Animals make use of signs without knowing that there are signs, Maritain noted—that is to say (1957: 53), "without perceiving the relation of signification".

"Perceiving", moreover, may be understood in several senses. There is at one level a purely sensory perception, distinct from and superordinate to (as containing and further specifying) external sensations. At this level the relation of signification can be grasped *in actu exercito*, that is to say, grasped in a practical way as employed in interaction to make one's way in the physical surroundings and especially to get control over them or turn them to one's advantage. There is at another level an intellectual perception, also containing the lower levels of sensory perception and external sensation in a superordinate way, and at this level the relation of signification can be not only used and manipulated *in actu exercito* but also distinguished from the vehicle conveying it and the object it conveys. It can be considered *in actu signato*, that is, directly and according to what is proper to it, not as an object directly experienced (for directly we experience only the objects related, sign vehicle on the one hand and object signified on the other hand, albeit as connecting in a single experience). This possibility, we will see, underlies anthroposemiosis in its difference from zoösemiosis. But first it will be necessary to achieve an understanding of relation in this abstract sense, only indirectly given in experience, and then to see how it applies to both zoösemiosis in the establishment of an Umwelt and to anthroposemiosis in the transformation, principally through language, of the biological Umwelt into the distinctively human Lebenswelt (if yet species-specific, at least no longer closed upon itself).

So we take up our question: In what sense is the parent of a dead child still a parent?

To answer this somewhat unpleasant question, let us begin by considering the notion of parenthood itself, a clearly relative form of being. It is early enough in the development of reproductive technology to confine our consideration here to the traditional form of parenthood, that which results from a sexual exchange between a male and a female of the species, as a result of which the female conceives and comes to term. At that moment, initially unknown to the couple responsible, they have become what formerly they were not, parents of this offspring.

Right away it is easy to see that "being a parent" or "becoming a parent", in the minimal sense, results from an action that is over and above the being of each of the individuals taken as independent biological organisms in their own right. It is true, of course, that there are also cultural notions of parent and parenthood that overlay and are in some degree detachable from this biologically rooted notion, according to which one may "be a parent" in the cultural sense by raising offspring not begotten by one's own sexual actions or "not be a parent" by failing to live up to the responsibilities ensuing from one's own sexual action. But the observing of these refinements serves here to make clear the more determinate and limited sense in which we are posing our question.

Thus, the being of a parent is identified with, but not identical with, the being of each or either of the two organisms begetting the child. Being a parent is an aspect of the being of both, a characteristic of the being of each of them, but not in the sense that each has an individual skin color, say, or weight.[12] This characteristic we are considering, newly acquired, attaches to the generating organisms not as independent individual organisms in their own right, nor even as dyadically interacting organisms, but only as organisms interacting in such a way as to have achieved, deliberately or not, "a third kind of being, consisting in and resulting from the coordination in time of two extremes", the generating pair taken together as one extreme (the unity of transitive action, "the act of the agent in the patient"), the child generated taken as the other. In short, the characteristic of being a parent rests not on the dynamic interaction of sexual activity alone but on that taken together with, coordinated with, a certain outcome that exists precisely as a trajectory independent of either parent in his or her individual being.

At the same time, the child is "their child", and they are "this child's parents", as it were, permanently. But, of course, all three may die, separately or together. What is permanent is not in the material and biological order but in the order of discourse and understanding. It is a matter of a truth, whether it be known or not, forgotten or remembered: that child was of those parents.

At a certain moment, the individual organisms existing unto themselves acquired as a permanent part of their being, not from the standpoint of existence, but from the standpoint of understanding, the quality of being parents of that child; and the child, from the first, had as a quality of its being, being the offspring of those parents. To be fully understood, the individuals who became parents must be understood with regard to the child, and the child, to be fully understood, must be known in relation to the parents.

Of course, on the side of existence, the parents are not a mere relation to the child, and the child is not a mere relation to the parents. Each exists in its own right, separate from the others. Nonetheless, although neither is the relation characterizing their being, neither can be fully known unless that relation be included.

Here we have the first and most general sense in which being is relative: according to the requirements of understanding. Within experience, every individual exists in such a way as to require being thought of in terms of things that the individual is not, in order to be understood for what the indiviudal is. This requirement transcends the independent aspect of the individual existent and in fact reveals that independent aspect to be itself dependent upon other factors, some present and still essential

---

12. "Relation does not depend on a subject in quite the same way that other determinations of being do", Poinsot observes (1632a: 89/13–17), "but stands rather as a third kind of being consisting in and resulting from the coordination in time of two extremes". Whence he concludes (89/18–20): "and therefore, in order to exist in the nature of things, the relation *continuously* depends on the fundament coordinating it with the terminus, and not only on a subject and a productive cause."

(like the atmosphere and gravity, for example) and others past and essential no longer to the individual existing before us (like the dead parents, say, or the prehistoric organisms that began the process of establishing an oxidizing atmosphere).

In the middle ages, the philosophers were mainly concerned with understanding and classifying the ways in which an individual could be said to be able to exist in its own right independent of our knowledge of that existence as a matter of individual or actual fact. They were disconcerted to find that certain aspects of even possible existence could not be reduced to a determinate classification, but invaded every possible determinate classification. To their credit, they did not simply trivialize or brush aside these discoveries, despite the fact that they were unwelcome in terms of their theoretical goal and anomalous to it. Instead, they established a rudimentary systematization of these vagrant aspects of being (*ens vagans*, they said, a rather colorful phrase) by assigning them the name of "transcendentals", that is, characteristics transcending any one determinate mode of possible existence in the physical order of being.

Later on, probably after Duns Scotus (c.1302–1303), this name of "transcendental" became transferred or extended to that intractable sense of relative being that turned out to pertain to the understanding of even the most independent modes of physical entities, and which previously (after Boethius, c.510) had been called only by the confused and confusing title of *relatio* or *relativum secundum dici*, what we have called being relative according to the requirements of discourse or understanding.

However, being a parent whose child is living proof here and now and being relative according to the requirements of discourse, are not the same thing. For the parent was relative in other ways according to the requirements of discourse before the child came along, and to this condition the child added something real. This addition was more than a mere new aspect of the organism become parent, more, that is, than an aspect permanently modifying the discursive demands of that organism-become-parent on an omniscient understanding (indeed, modification of this sort the sexual intercourse alone, without any issue of offspring, would have achieved!). The relativity according to the requirements of discourse is permanent in a way that the prospective nurturing relation between parent and offspring is not. For this relation, both must exist; for the former or transcendental relation, continued existence is not necessary.

So there is a second sort of relative being, one that is not identified with either side of a related pair but that exists between them and exists in no other way. This relation may or may not be known. For example, a male may engage in a sexual relation that results in an offspring only after he is no longer around to know about it. In such a case, the child is determinately the child of this parent, even though the parent does not know he is a parent and the child may never know who its parent is or was. In such a case, while both father and offspring exist, the relation between them is independent of being determinately known, as is proved by the neither of them determinately knowing it, but is nonetheless determinate between them: that one is the father of this child, this child is the offspring of that parent. The relation is purely physical.

In the more acceptable case, where the offspring is both known and nurtured by the parent, the physical relation is objective as well as physical. That is to say, it is recognized as existing as well as existing. This relation, objective and physical or merely physical, is distinct from and superordinate to the individual being of both parent and child. It is not merely that intelligible aspect proper to the individual being of both whereby, henceforward, in order to be fully understood, each must be thought in connection with the other. Unlike this permanent aspect of intelligibility, the physical relation and the objectivity that may or may not accompany it are transitive: they are a type of relation that comes into being for a while and then ceases or, in the case of the objective relation, that may pass in and out of being many times, in each case remaining as a relation unchanged in its essential content.

Moreover, when the child is not only of this parent but known to be of this parent, the physical and the objective relation are the same. This is never true of the transcendental relation. The relation whereby *this* organism must be understood (if it is to be fully understood, which of course it need not: it is a question of an ideal requirement which becomes actual to the extent full understanding is accomplished) as parent of that organism is never the same as the relation whereby *that* organism is to be understood as child of this parent. For the transcendental relation in each case belongs to the individual being in what of it is not the other individual. Poinsot summarized the point thus (1632a: 90/23–27): "a transcendental relation is not a form adventitious to a subject or absolute thing, but something imbibed thereto, while connoting something extrinsic upon which the subject depends or with which it was engaged". In short (ibid. 90/33–37):

> A transcendental relation is in the subjective entity itself and does not differ from its subjective being, and so its whole being is not respecting another, which is what is required for a relation according to its being.

It is, therefore, a question of two different ways in which relativity can be exercised. One way is identical with the subjective being of an individual and part and parcel with it, and a second way is over and above the subjective being of the individual precisely as the actual connection here and now is realized between one subject and another. Relativity in the first sense, transcendental relation, is identical with the possibility for understanding a being.

Relativity in the second sense, to which we have yet to assign a distinct name, is identical with the actual connection between two subjective entities here and now, whether that connection be physical or objective. When a being which is the parent of a child is also known to be the parent of that child, the relation between the parent and the child is both physical and objective. If the child dies, the physical relation between them ceases, but it remains that the erstwhile parent must be *thought of* as having been the parent of that child if the parent is to be understood according to the full extent of its intelligible being. When the parent is not only knowable as parent of the child now dead (i.e., transcendentally relative), but is here and now thought of in relation to the now dead child, the once physical relation is now re-established in an objective way: the parent is not only thinkable in truth relative to that child, but actually thought in relation to that child. The relative in the first sense is in itself "something absolute on which follows or could follow" a relative in the second sense, which is the difference between something that is relative in the transcendental sense and something relative as a relation purely and strictly so called.[13]

We see then that transcendental relation captures the realization that everything that exists does so through a series of interactions. Some of these interactions preceded the now existing thing; other of the interactions are ones the thing itself is engaged in; and yet other of the interactions are consequent upon those that the thing itself is engaged in, although it is not itself engaged directly in those consequences, either because it is there and then elsewhere engaged or because it has itself ceased to be, period. On the other hand, there are the relations themselves attendant upon all these interactions. They are, comparatively speaking, ethereal. They are not the related things; they are the relations themselves. They are not in the things; they are between them. Yet they exist, physically when not known, objectively when known, objectively and physically when the knowing and the beings related temporally coincide, purely ob-

---

13. Poinsot expands on this technical but crucial point of difference as follows (1632a: 89/32–90/9): "The exercise or rationale of a relation according to the way something must be expressed in discourse is not purely to respect a terminus, but to exercise something else *whence a relation could follow*. And for this reason St. Thomas well said (c.1252–1256: 2. dist. 1. q. 1. art. 5. reply to obj. 8) that these, the transcendental relatives, involve a fundament *and* a relation, whereas what are relative according to being express *only* a relation, as can be gleaned from the readily seen fact that transcendental relatives bear on a terminus rather by founding a relation than by actually respecting, and for that reason do not respect the terminus in question in its pure character as a terminus of a relation but according to some other rationale, such as that of a cause, or of an effect, or of an object, or the like. So a relation according to the way being must be expressed in discourse is constantly distinguished . . . from relation according to the way relation has being in that the principal significate of an expression conveying a relation according to the way a subject must be expressed in discourse is not a relation, but something else, upon which a relation follows. But when the principal significate of some expression is the relation itself, and not something absolute, then there is a relation according to the way what is signified has being."

jectively when the two diverge, either through the passage of time (objective historical relations) or because the relations conceived have not yet existed (a future machine) or cannot exist physically in the way that they are conceived (nine-foot insects on the surface of this planet). Transcendental relations are not relations strictly and properly but comparative requirements of action and intelligibility. What are the relations strictly and properly is that which is consequent upon the interactions or actual understandings not as effects but as the patterns according to which effects eventuate and causes act. Thus, parenthood is a relation, but a parent is an agent, and a child is an effect. The foundation of the relation of parenthood in any given case is a determinate outcome of a determinate action, but the relation itself is neither the contingent action nor its determinate outcome. The relation is the pattern, the thirdness, linking the two and superordinate to each.

Let us expand our example for a moment, choosing an illustration no less concrete but even more homely. Consider a room with all its furnishings piled in the center, and that same room with these same furnishings tastefully arranged. Not one *thing* in the room is different in the two cases, only *what is between the things*, namely, their pattern or arrangement. Yet what a difference in the room. And the difference is a genuine difference; it is a "physical" difference in our sense.[14] Moreover, the relations cannot be changed directly. Only the things in the room can be directly acted upon, whence the change in the relations follows.

We see then what is singular about the being of relations in the strict sense: when a physical individual or any subjective aspect of a material being is conceived in the mind, what is conceived is not that individual as it exists apart from the mind but precisely that individual in relation to the conception. But, when I conceive of a physical relation strictly as such, both what exists apart from the thinking and what exists through the thinking are identical, are relations in the same sense. A subjective mode of being objectively represented in the mind is in principle other than the represented thing, even though and when the two may coincide: Homer I know in thought, others knew him in person as well; the centaur I know in thought as well as any other man knows the centaur. But an intersubjective mode of being objectively represented is in principle no other

---

14. Here I follow the tradition of Aquinas and Poinsot, wherein the term "physical" extends to the entire order of beings able to exist independently of human thought, from the humblest material entities to the loftiest of supposed spirits, including even the divinity in its proper life (see, for example, Poinsot 1637: 38). As noted in Deely 1988: 97, reviews of my 1985 edition of Poinsot's *Tractatus de Signis* (Furton 1985, Henry 1987, and others) demonstrated the widespread ignorance in contemporary scholarship of this technical but important point of late Latin philosophical usage. Reviewers repeatedly criticized the translation of *realis* as "physical" on the ground that, for the medievals, *realis* applied to spiritual beings (what Henry calls "theological entities") as well as to natural and material beings; whence they asserted—wrongly—that *physicum* and its derivates are not applicable in such a context.

than the thing it is represented to be. Both what is thought and the basis on which it is thought, both what is apart from the mind and what is conceived in the mind, are relations in the same sense, are in their content identical, even though and when the two may diverge.

This is a point that seems first to have been made explicitly by Cajetan (1507: in 1. 28. art. 1. par. 9):

> Relation is the one type of being for which the qualification "existing in the mind" does not detract from what is proper to it, as this qualification does detract from what is proper to every other type of being. For a rose formed by thought is not a rose, nor is Homer in opinion Homer; but a relation formed by the mind is a true relation.
>
> Nor is the distinction between a rose in physical existence and a rose in objective existence a distinction of essentially diverse entities, of which the one is a mind-independent being and the other a mind-dependent being, as we have said occurs with relations: it is a distinction rather of one and the same essential type according to two different ways of existing, namely, in itself subjectively or in knowledge relatively.

How this point is essential to semiotic we shall shortly see. At this juncture, what needs to be noted is how the being of experience divides respecting the notion of being relative into the subjectively or *intra*subjectively relative and the pure or *inter*subjective mode of relative being. And what is unique to the right hand of the division also needs to be noted, namely, that intersubjectively relative being alone is indifferent to having its ground or "cause" in the broadest sense in thought or in dynamic interactions: whether a strict relation is physical only, objective only, or a mixture of both, what it is in itself and what it is in conception remains exactly the same, to wit, a connection or actual nexus, a pattern, joining what is otherwise diverse.[15] Since it is a question of being at this point,

---

15. This unique feature of intersubjectively relative being explains why the odd case of a self-relation, "Jones ate with Jones", where the Jones eating and the Jones eaten with are the same Jones—that is, Jones ate alone—was regarded by the scholastics as the paradigm case of a purely objective relation, despite the identity status (in Peircean terms) of both subject and terminus (cf. Peirce c.1890: 1.365 p. 190). For the requirement for a relation that its foundation be distinct from its terminus is here met only through the rational activity of the mind itself reduplicating its object through a relation which, outside of thought, i.e., physically, cannot obtain as a relation but only as a subjective mode of being, i.e., Jones' being himself. Poinsot puts it thus (1632a: 70/43–71/10): "In the case of mind-dependent relations, their actual existence consists in actually being cognized objectively, which is something that does not take its origin from the fundament and terminus, but from the understanding. Whence many things could be said of a subject"—either as a physical given in the environment independently of the discourse wherein the objective relation is formed, or as a strictly objective subject to begin with (such as that a given word is an adjective, contains five letters, is used substantively, or is identical with itself, etc.)—"without the resultance of the relation" either supervenient upon the subject in physical existence or the relation in which the signification of a linguistic element consists—"because this does not follow upon the fundament itself and the terminus, but upon cognition; whereas in the case of mind-independent or physical relations, since the relation results automatically from the fundament and the terminus, nothing

and of the being, as we shall see, whence semiosis is possible as a fact of nature, we are at an appropriate point to suggest the name "ontological relation" for that pure form of intersubjective being that is indifferently physical or objective and contrasts in what is proper to it with the various forms of intrasubjective being otherwise making up the physical order of "transcendental relation" in its full extent.[16] The trick is to remember that the transcendental relation denotes what is not a relation (an individual or inherent characteristic modifying an individual) as it connotes a relation between the individual denoted and some other individual(s) or event(s), while the connoted relation denotatively taken would be an ontological relation rather than a transcendental one.[17]

In other words, in the classical terminology of *subject* of a relation, *terminus* of a relation, and *foundation* or ground of a relation (the basis on which subject and terminus are related), the transcendental relation covers the subject of the relation precisely as founding the relation and also the term of the relation in whatever other aspects it may have over and above that of being a terminus purely and strictly, whereas the ontological relation covers strictly *the relation itself* as an intersubjective mode or pattern between subject and terminus whence they are caught up in common (Poinsot 1632a: 84/45–85/19):

> A relation accrues to a subject without any change that is directly and immediately terminated at the relation, but not without a change that is terminated mediately and indirectly at that relation. Just as risibility results from the same action by which a man is produced, so from the production of a white thing is produced similitude to another existing white thing. But if another white thing did not exist, by virtue of the generation of the first white thing that similitude and any other relation that would result from the positing of its terminus would remain in a virtual state. Whence distance neither

---

belongs in an order to a terminus by virtue of a fundament except by the medium of the relation".

16. Thus the notion of "relative being" is rendered synonymous with the notion of *finite being*, and subdivides into the order of subjectivity as *intra*subjectively relative being, which embraces individuals and all their inherent characteristics or modifications, and the order of intersubjectivity or *inter*subjectively relative being, which embraces all and only those pure beings-toward which arise over and above but dependent upon individuals with their inherent characteristics, uniting them in a network or web of communication of various levels and types. The characterization of the transcendental relation as intrasubjective, which I adopt here (in contrast to the ontological relation as intersubjective), was suggested by Julio Pinto in a mini-course we jointly conducted on the campus of the Pontificia Universidade Católica de São Paulo during the week of 22–26 May 1989 for the Associação Brasileira de Semiótica: Regional São Paulo.

17. Notice that the terms "denotation" and "connotation" are used in their proper traditional Latin sense and not in the corrupted sense introduced by Mill. The sense of the terms introduced by Mill as a "tax upon credulity" (in Peirce's colorful denunciation, 1867a: 2.393) and which yet remains popular in both logical and (especially) literary circles today is, as Peirce rightly says, objectionable and deserving of being abandoned.

conduces to nor obstructs the resultance of a pure relation, because these relations do not depend upon a local situation; for near or far, a son is in the same way the son of his father. Nor is the relation in the other extreme produced by the terminus itself through some emission of power when it is brought into existence. Rather is the existence of the terminus the condition for a relation's resulting from an already existing fundament by virtue of the original generation whereby that fundament was brought into being as inclining toward any terminus of such a fundament. Whence even though the generating has now ceased, it yet remains in its effect or power, inasmuch as it leaves a fundament sufficient for a relation to result.

We see then what is peculiar about the notion of relative being taken in its full extension thus divided: it includes everything that falls within our experience and so is difficult to grasp precisely because the implied term of opposition—nonrelative being, or absolute being—is at the concrete level a phantom of the mind, like the notion of "nonbeing" in general. It is not a question of some beings that are relative and other beings that are not relative, but a question rather of beings all of which are relative, though relative in two sharply contrasting though connected senses: Every being that exists in its own right is, by virtue of that very fact, subjectively relative throughout its existence; but, in addition to this subjective relativity according to which a being proximately depends on some things more than others and influences some things but not others, etc., there is the further relativity according to which the subjects are here and now intersubjectively connected actually to this thing rather than that, and later to another rather than to this, until such time as they cease to be. There is, in short, a twofold dimension or level to the relativity of being: on the one hand, there is an *underlay* of subjective relativity according to which everything ultimately implies everything else but not in equally direct or proximate ways at the level of possibility or intelligibility, even though everything is not actually related to everything else at the level of existence and physical interaction; and, on the other hand, there is at the same time an *overlay* of intersubjective relations, both physical and objective, according to which some things are actually interactive with some things but not with others in this or that way.

We are now in a position to answer our question about the living parent whose child has died. The parent remains a parent at the level of transcendental relation, while ceasing to be a parent at the level of physical relation, although this physical relation continues to exist objectively to the extent that the parent or anyone else thinks about it. The same relation formed now only in thought formerly existed also physically, and it is by virtue of that same relation that the parent is a parent.

Of course, if, as happens, a supposed father, say, was deceived into thinking that a child was his when in fact it was begotten by another, the objective relation according to which he was called and thought to be, perhaps even by the child, "father", continues without ceasing in any sense upon the death of the child. It is thus by the relation on its physical side that the father is in fact the father, while it is by that same relation (or by what is thought to be that relation even though it is in fact a different relation owing to the nonexistence of a physical relation for the objective relation to be the same as) that the father is called "father". Thus is the truth of dicisigns a consequence of the relations they embody according to whether what is asserted objectively coincides with or deviates from what exists relative to another order of being than the objective.

This peculiarity of ontological relation—whereby it, and it alone in the whole of physical reality, is indifferent to the source or ground of its being—underlies semiosis as a unique type of activity in nature. The same relation or set of relations that exists at one time purely objectively may be transferred as such into the order of physical being. When this happens, the physical order itself is reorganized and realizes possibilities that previously were remote rather than proximate and actual. This, as we will consider in chapter 6, is what happens throughout physiosemiosis, as a given environment becomes modified more and more in the direction of being hospitable to life, and then subsequently still further in the direction of more and more complex or "higher" forms of life.[18] Here it will be enough to show how the ontological singularity unique to relation in the order of physical being provides the ground for the prior possibility of semiosis at the level of the experience of organisms, which is our main concern here, inasmuch as, as we have already seen, it is at the upper levels of biosemiosis that the basic concepts of semiotics have been fully established.

The common ground of biosemiosis lies in what used to be called "natural signs", but what is now more commonly divided, after Peirce, into indices, icons, and symbols (although of course not all icons or symbols are natural signs, either). A footprint in the sand is indexical of a person's passing, and of the direction of the passing, unless the footprints be the skillful work of a man passing east in such a way as to leave the impression of a man passing west, in which event the footprints remain indexically accurate to a degree but iconically misleading in another degree, and are in fact symbols of an exceptional skill.

---

18. The causality or action of signs may in this way intersect with and, if so, objectively channel anything of final causality that might be at work in the physical environment. But the action proper to signs remains extrinsic to and objectively distinct from this final causality. Ralph Powell's demonstration of the confusion in this regard in Peirce's writings (Powell 1986, 1988) should, therefore, be regarded as a guidepost in contemporary development of the doctrine of signs, demarcating one of the major areas in which textual exegesis needs to be clearly subordinated to fundamental research and analysis of the requirements of the problems involved.

Natural signs are essential to the survival of most if not all species of animals. They need to be taken for what they are, or, in the reverse case, mistaken for what they are intended to be mistaken for, if the animal in question is to secure its food. What happens in such a case? Precisely that the foundation for a physical relation is taken or mistaken for a corresponding objective relation, as a result of which food is provided or safety secured.

The relation of clouds to rain is a relation of cause and effect. When that relation has also been experienced, an interpretant becomes established. What was formerly a mere physical relation, a relation of secondness, acquires now, through the interpretant, a thirdness whereby that same relation functions also semiotically. Because the physical relationship as such need only be dyadic, whereas the semiotic relationship is necessarily triadic, there is the possibility of error, or misinterpretation. There is also the possibility of deception. The objective world wherein actual semiosis transpires is only occasionally the same and in large part different from the physical environment. But to the extent that it is the same, to the extent that it overlaps—and this is the extent to which every species depends for its survival on food, which is a considerable extent—that extent and that overlap result from the indifference of intersubjective being to the difference between what is objective and what is physical, as we have seen.

Thus, it is the being proper to relation that is also the being proper to signs, even though relations properly speaking need not be semiosic relations. Not all relations in the ontological sense pass through actual experience, but all relations in the ontological sense are indifferent to the order of physical existence, such that, once taken up into actual experience, they also take on an objective life relatively independent of physical being. It is in this way that they provide the raw material of biosemiosis. The actual being proper to the sign is the being of an ontological relation taken up into the experience of an organism, whether directly from the biological heritage of that organism (so-called "instinctive notions") or culled rather from individual experience, where it serves to connect objectively perceptual and sensory elements. The action of signs first arises precisely from physically related environmental factors coming to be seen objectively as related, and, conversely, from objectively related factors being presented as physically related. The uniqueness of semiosis as an activity and the detached and ambiguous quality it has as an action results from the being peculiar and proper to the ontological relation whereby, as we have seen, it can be neither directly altered nor directly perceived. The permeability of relation as such to realization in either the physical or the objective order also makes the two indistinguishable in direct experience. This is a matter not of confusion but of the reality proper to experience, wherein the objective and the physical are intertwined in the sign. This permeability is why the natural sign provides a common denominator in biosemiosis, even though it can be natural in different ways for different species.

An example of a natural sign unique to the level of anthroposemiosis may help to grasp the general point at stake here. Let us consider the case of a fossil bone. This bone may or may not be known to exist. If not, let us suppose it yet belongs to a class of bones well established among those expert in the Pleistocene. One day the bone is uncovered, but by a gardener, not a paleontologist. Since the bone is in an advanced state of fossilization, let us suppose that our gardener does not even recognize it as a bone, let alone a fossil bone. For that, a more developed interpretant is required, one proportioned more exactly to what the bone relates to in its living past. Nevertheless, a fossil bone is just what it is. Such an interpretant as is required for its recognition nowhere existed actually in the middle ages, let us say, but now, among our postulated Pleistocene specialists, it exists indeed as a common property.

What is this interpretant? Certainly not an idea psychologically considered. It is rather an idea in the semiotic sense, moreover as fashioned publically through the training of paleontologists, such that those who have by training acquired it possess in their minds a foundation or "fundament" whence will result or "dimanate", under appropriate conditions, a network of relations including that bone.[19] But first, one of them at least will have to see the bone in question.

Supposing that occurs. Supposing that one of our students of the Pleistocene visits our gardener just as the gardener is about to deposit into a trash bin the bone which had irritatingly obstructed his gardening. "What is that you have there?" Now our gardener, being also a student of Peirce, may at this point respond, casually tossing the bone toward the trash, "A brute fact at the level of secondness."

But our paleontologist had not asked her question idly. She had spoken out of a glimmer of suspicion, a hint of recognition, as it were—she was voicing in context a low-risk abductive gamble. Into the brute fact at the level of secondness something of thirdness had already, thanks to her training, begun to enter. "Let me have a closer look", she said, moving

---

19. As an additional exercise, but one not requisite for grasping the discussion to follow, the reader may profit from trying to envisage the situation in light of the following text from Poinsot (1632a: 388/38–46), commenting on an analogous situation: "And that a previously merely potential relation should spring from a fundament actually, or that a relation therefrom already in existence would be extended or expanded by applying itself to a newly posited terminus as pertaining to the already existent relationship as such, is something intrinsic to the being proper to relation taken ontologically as such—namely, to tend and to be determined in act toward that in respect of which the relation was already tending virtually, and only for want of an existent terminus was not anchored in being independently of being cognized." Those interested in the full details of these technical doctrinal points are referred to the more specialized discussion in Deely 1988: 56–87, esp. 56–68.

toward the bone discarded as a peculiarly shaped rock. "This", she announces on careful inspection, "is no rock. This is a rare fossil bone, which just may revolutionize a bit of our understanding of the Pleistocene in this area." Whereupon, clutching the bone with great excitement, she ran off in the direction of the university.

What has happened here? A physical relation, recognized for what it had been, thanks to the dynamic interaction of its fundament (the bone) producing physical changes in the student of paleontology's optic nerves, became at the same moment also a sign of what had been. A transcendental relation, the bone of a dinosaur, which once had a physical relation to that dinosaur, but no more (the dinosaur being dead), yet gave rise to an objective relation corresponding somewhat with the physical relation that had been. The gardener's rock had become the paleontologist's sign.

5

Zoösemiotics and Anthroposemiotics

CLASSICAL PHILOSOPHY had much to say about Aristotle's definition of the human being as a "rational animal". The problem was that, in this definition, the term "animal" was somehow never quite taken seriously, and most of the discussion centered on showing how "being rational" contrasted with "being animal" in such a way as to render animality unimportant. In the extreme case—the work of Descartes (1637, 1641)—the contrast was emphasized to the extent of being transformed into an outright opposition, and a new definition of the human as a "thinking thing" was proposed to replace the old definition entirely.

"Thinking things"—humans—were opposed to "extended things"—all bodies, including the animals other than human. In this way, the ancient definition was bifurcated: the first part (which supposedly designated a uniquely human factor in one among the animals) became the whole definition of the human being, while the second part (which supposedly designated something shared by human beings with other species or types of cognitive animate beings) was made to reduce those other types of beings to a material uniformity that became the whole definition of what was opposed to the human and in contrast with it, namely, bodies of whatever sort.

This modern dualism of mind and body was rooted in a certain interpretation of the mind's ideas as being themselves the objects directly given in experience. As we will see, the idea thus interpreted as an objective representation—as an object before being a sign—is incompatible with the interpretation of ideas as signs. A suspicion of this incompatibility, indeed, may have been the reason why Locke, in proposing the introduction of semiotic into the scheme of human knowledge, saw as a first task for semiotic the bringing of "ideas"—the inner side of knowing—along with "words"—the outer manifestation of the knowing—into the perspective of the sign. For he rightly guessed that the successful completion of this task would result in a radically different account of knowledge and experience than what was developing in the then-modern philosophy, including his own.

The semiotic understanding of what a human being is can only be an upshot of that radically different account. If we are to propose, for example, "linguistic animal" as a semiotic definition, we will find that, in order to interpret the defining terms semiotically, we cannot avoid taking animality very seriously indeed, if only in order to understand language. What comes first in the expression, we will find, comes second in the interpretation of the expression. For in the expression, "linguistic animal", the linguistic term not only presupposes for its sense what is first of all an animal construction, namely, an Umwelt, but also differentiates the objective relations comprising an Umwelt not from above, independently, or externally, but from within.

A. The Content of Experience

Although belonging to the cognitive dimension of experience, semiotics does not have its roots in a theory first of all. First of all it is rooted in a process, the process of semiosis, specifically as that process is responsible for the very possibility and for whatever there is of actuality in the experience of any living being. This actuality, in certain cases (such as our own), can then be reflected upon and come to constitute in its own right an object according to what is specific to it, namely, the dependency of experience throughout on the action of signs. At that moment of reflective insight, semiotics begins as a moment of anthroposemiosis.

Like any other work of reflection, the development of semiotics is subject to errors, false starts, and blind alleys. At the outset, perhaps the single problem that has most often thrown off reflections on the sign has been getting straight the distinction between a sign and a representation and, consequently, the difference between signification and representation. We have touched on this distinction in chapter 4 particularly, but here some further remarks will be helpful. The confusion comes from the fact that every sign must be a representation, but, whereas every signification involves representation, not every representation must be a sign. In other words, the sign is a representation of a certain type but of a certain type only, whereas a representation may or may not be a sign.

A representation may be of itself, or it may be of something other than itself. In the former case it constitutes an object, but only in the latter case does it constitute a sign. This is why, as we have seen in chapter 4, the sign in its proper—its irreducible—being always involves a pure relationship. In the technical terms established there, we may say that a representation as such may be a merely transcendental relationship, whereas a sign is also always an ontological relation. In the sign, the transcendental element of the relation—the representational factor— is merely fundamental, that is, the foundation or ground whence springs the ontological relation to something else—the significate or signified. And it is in this relation to another that the sign formally consists.

In the case of a representation as such, what is fundamental and what is formal may coincide (the case of objective self-representation). When that occurs, the representation exists as an object of awareness. But, in the case of a sign, what is fundamental (the representation grounding and founding the relation of signification) and what is formal (the relation of signification itself) never coincide. It is a question of modality, as I have explained in technical discussions elsewhere (esp. 1986e: 39–40). As a result, although an object may also function experientially as a sign, it need not so function (the moon, well known to ancient man, never served for him as a reminder of the U.S. Apollo Space Program of the 1970s, nor need the god Apollo and the moon have been brought together in order to signify a program to reach the moon). And a sign that is also an object may, accordingly, cease to be sign in any given respect for any given case or instance of perception (as when we tie a string to remind us of something and then forget what the string is to remind us of, or when we can't remember a word we have previously looked up, and so forth).

The confusion of signs as such with representations has been, historically, perhaps the most common cause of misunderstanding of the role of signs in experience. This confusion is what led Descartes and Locke to posit ideas as the objects of our awareness and then to trouble themselves mightily with the problem of figuring out how these self-representations might or might not be causally connected with or resemblant of the assumed (but not directly experienced) existence of extramental things. Once it is understood, however, that objects as such are always representations but representations as such are never signs, it becomes clear that, to whatever extent ideas are signs, they are differentiated from, rather than identified with, the objects of our awareness here and now. The distinction between representation and sign, in what concerns semiotics, is the distinction between object and sign. A representation may or may not be an object, but to be an object is necessarily to be a representation, while for being a sign being a representation is not enough.

These are extremely important distinctions, the full understanding of which involves not a few subtleties. The point of entry into a semiotic understanding of ideas as signs is the point of exit from the modern interpretation of ideas as representations, as the objects of which we are directly aware when we think. Precisely as signs, ideas are separated from rather than identified with the objects they signify, and objects signified that in turn become signs do so by themselves becoming differentiated from what they signify. As signified, objects always presuppose a relation to something other than themselves on which their being as objects depends, for, as objects, they exist precisely as cognized. Indeed, their being as object is at the terminus completing such a relation.

The foundation of such an objective relation, however—the element of representation in the signifying—need by no means be itself an object, nor could it be in every case. For the being of objects represented as other than what does the representing implies among the representing elements some at least that lay the ground of objectivity without themselves being part of that direct ground. The experience of objects that in turn signify other objects must not be allowed to obscure this fundamental point, if the standpoint of semiotic is to be achieved. This is a second subtlety on which integral achievement of the semiotic point of view very much depends.

The need for an objectively sensible element as sign-vehicle is not essential to the functioning of the sign as such, but only to the transformation of objects already known in their own right into signs of other objects as well. The essential function of the sign, however, has already been achieved in the making present of the object in the first place. For, in that case, the intraorganismic factor (the psychological state, say, or the nervous condition) on the basis of which the object exists as known to begin with, is already serving to engender the relation whereby the factor in question serves to make present in awareness that which it itself is not, namely, the object. The object may itself then *in turn* also function as a sign of other objects or be taken inferentially as a "reverse sign" to abduce the existence of its corresponding idea or psychological state on the basis of which it exists here and now as something experienced or known. But the signs at the base of objectivity never present themselves directly as objects. This is a simple matter of fact, whose possibility is explained (the reason for the possibility of which is given) by the being of the sign as essentially relational over and above the subjectivity of whatever is related by it, as we saw in Chapter 4.

The objects of experience as such, thus, depend in every case on signs, and they themselves further differentiate within experience into other signs, so that one object, which as object represents itself, comes also through associations of various kinds to represent other objects besides itself. In that way, an object comes to be a sign as well as an object in its own right.

But it is not only into signs that objects dissolve through experience. They also dissolve (or resolve) into objects of very different types. Here we come to a third subtlety on which a grasp of the main entry point into semiotics depends: just as signs are prior to and distinct from objects within experience, so objects are prior to and distinct from the things with which they happen to be partially identical. At the most primitive levels of experience, and throughout the most sophisticated experiences, no doubt certain elements of objectivity are also prejacent elements of the physical surroundings. But it is not as prejacent that they are objective. As prejacent, in their prejacency, they were not objective in our sense at all. Whatever is objective exists through an actual representation, that is, as cognized or known. If what exists as known also happens to exist, in whole or in part, physically as well, that is, independently of the cognizing, then we say that it is, besides being an object, also a thing—a case of a "physical object". Thus, within our experience, things are included both among objects and among what objects may become signs of. But objects may also be and become signs of non-things, of mistakes, errors, lies, wishes, or fantasies of various kinds, including realizable dreams of a better future than what is existing could alone portend. Whatever is known is, as such—that is, as known—objective, be it Hamlet or Napoleon. But whatever exists objectively may (as in the case of Hamlet) or may not (as in the case of Napoleon) exist *only* objectively.

We are not, therefore, going beyond the boundaries of experience by introducing here the notion of "thing", for precisely within those boundaries some among objects present themselves as having an existence that exceeds the knowing of it. The notion of things in its contrast both to objects and to signs arises inevitably and quite early in the experience of each of us, through the resistance we meet to our desires and, indeed, our expectations, with such regularity that there is no adult real or conceivable who does not have the idea of an environment surrounding him or her that is comprised of a great variety of objects possessing a being or existence that exceeds the individual's experience of them, in precisely the sense that much of this variety anteceded the individual me, much of it is unknown to me (it is full of surprises, welcome and unwelcome), and much of it will survive my demise.

Things, in this most general sense, are whatever in my experience is experienced as not reducing to my experience of it, and as having an embodiment, moreover, in the environmental structures such that it is not a mere figment of thought or imagination, but has also an existence proper to itself that is physical or "real" in the sense that it obtains apart from my thinking of it. Things have bodies, in a word.

But note, too, the transformation semiotics imposes on our use of the common term "objective". The word "object" and its derivatives need to be appropriated from common usage to become *termini technici* in the context of semiotics. "Object" or "objective structure" refer, in contrast to the various usual usages, to the becoming of things through and in experience. Objects are *not* what things are in a being prior to and independent of experience. Objects *are* what the things become once experienced—that is, once they take on the existence proper to experience. But objects *are not* only things experienced. Objects are more than things, even when—which is not always the case—they are also things. Objects always involve a "relation to an observer", so to speak, or, more exactly, to an organism experiencing. Things only sometimes involve such a relation.

Within experience, the status of objects not designated to be signs with other objects so designated is peculiarly unstable, not because of a deficiency in the sign but because of an instability in the status of the object as such. This instability characterizes the object, regardless of whether a given object (a star, say, or a vampire) is also a prejacent physical element in the environment, whereby, as we have seen, every type of object, every objectivity and objective structure as fitted into experience, owes its being to the sign. The seemingly derivative and unstable status of signs that are objectively constituted within the order of experience, then, is due to the fact that any object can become a sign of any other object, and every object in experience begins as or quickly becomes a sign of several other objects (which ones depending on context and changing over time).

There remains, however, a constancy underlying this apparent variance. What does not change, what remains invariant at the base of experience, is the role of the sign as giving being to objects of whatever type in the first place, and providing the medium for their growth and transformations.

Thus, when we speak from the strict standpoint of experience (which of course we must in all contexts where we hope to avoid delusion), the sign is not by any means one thing among many others: the sign is not any thing at all, nor is it even first of all a distinct class of objects. As a type of object or objective structure contrasting with other objective structures, the sign is singularly unstable and derivative, for it is what all things—not just some—become in experience. But first of all and most radically, a sign is neither a thing nor an object but the pattern according to which things and objects interweave to make up the fabric of experience, wherein one part so stands for other parts as to give greater or lesser "meaning" to the whole at various times and in various contexts.

This status of the sign—whereby it is itself not a sensible or perceptible item (even when it has such an item for its foundation or "vehicle") but the arrangement of such items according to what they signify and provide as the content of significance to experienced objects—is, we shall see, the key to the higher level process of linguistic semiosis, which, as we shall also see, draws the line between human life forms and the other animals. Making this intelligible but imperceptible and insensible status itself objectified, thereby introducing into objects the dimension of stipulability, as we shall see, is precisely what constitutes anthroposemiosis in its difference from zoösemiosis and marks the beginning of language (prior to its exaptation for communication, for example, in speech) as a distinctive modeling system.[20]

But in order to develop this point effectively, we need first to develop more integrally the notion of embodiment as a fundamental objective structure. We saw above that the notion of having a body is proper to that type of object that is also a thing. But not only things have bodies. Embodiment is a general phenomenon of experience, inasmuch as whatever we encounter, learn, or share through experience has about it an aspect which is accessible by some sensory modality, be it only the physical being of marks or sounds subsumed within language and employed to create some text (a literary *corpus*, we even say). Herein resides and is conveyed some object of consideration that (we learn on occasion, whereas at other times we know—or think we know—from the start) has no other body besides a textual one. Examples are the medieval unicorn, the ancient minotaur, the celestial spheres which gave occasion for the condemnation and imprisonment of Galileo.

This was what we meant above in distinguishing, within our notion of objects experienced as things, the notion also of objects that may or may not be things. A thing experienced and an object of experience are not wholly the same. Of course, every thing *experienced* is by that very fact *also* an object of experience. But not every object of experience, by any means, is also a thing in the sense of having—such as experience indicates to be the case with much of nature—an existence prejacent to the human community and independent of an embodiment within that community.

Illustrative of this distinction are objects that are sometimes identical with physical things, as "the north star" names a unique natural entity contextualized to a specifically cultural but also magnetic and planetary

---

20. Edward T. Hall (1976: 57) remarks that "language is not (as is commonly thought) a system for transferring thoughts or meaning from one brain to another, but a system for organizing information and releasing thoughts and responses in other organisms. The materials for whatever insights there are in this world exist in incipient form, frequently unformulated but nevertheless already there in man. One may help to release them in a variety of ways, but it is impossible to plant them in the minds of others. Experience does that for us instead . . .". What we are asking is what must the construction of experience be in order to provide the materials of insight language is exapted to release in others?

frame of reference. At other times objects are identified with physical things without achieving a unique identity therewith—as the boundary for a certain stretch between Iowa and Illinois "is" the Mississippi River or as the President of the United States was first identified with Washington and later with a whole string of successors. At other times physical structures are made to instantiate objectivity without by any means being identical with the object locally embodied, as a statue of Romulus and Remus as founders of Rome, or a statue of the minotaur, has the physical aspect of a thing without that physical aspect being at all what is proper to its objectivity, in contrast to the mountain stream which enters experience as an object with a physical being precisely proper to and part and parcel of its objectivity. So, too, many objects of experience have no physical existence in addition to their embodiment within texts. Cinderella, we think, along with her glass slipper and pumpkin coach, are purely objective, in a way the rocks and stars are not. The celestial spheres, long thought to embody the very stars, turn out not to embody them at all. The stars proved to be the bodies, and the spheres proved to be but objects in the merest sense of fictions cut out of the whole cloth of experience by the understanding, which confused their objectivity with the physical existence proper to things become object, that is, experienced.

We the better see thus that the world of experience as experienced is through and through objective, the leprechaun no less than the cancer cell or silver bullet (used to kill werewolves) or mountain stream. We see, too, that the physical universe on its material side exists within and as part of the objective universe of experience, indeed, as its lining and skeleton, so to speak. But we see also that the objective and physical worlds are by no means coterminous, as each extends in its own way well beyond the confines of the other.

Of course, strictly speaking, only the objective world, in all its diversity mixed with physicality, exists as experienced. The physical surroundings may or may not also so exist—that is, objectively, or as experienced—and then only partially. At least, this is the notion of physical being and existence that experience imposes on each of us, the notion that there is more to what we experience in its aspect of embodiment than reduces down to our experience of it, so that there are no doubt "things we have yet to learn and things we may never know".

A particularly interesting aspect of the requirement that objects have an embodiment, be it only "textual" or linguistic in the sense of conveyance by some sensible *moyen* subsumed into the order of language, comes into view in those cases where the objects discoursed about are by definition independent of the world of bodies entirely: the case of supposed spirits or of the angels and deity of Western religious conviction. Here the objective embodiment—the texts explaining and arguing about the nature and reality of these beings—is precisely denied to be of the essence of the object experienced through the discourse about it. This case is in sharp contrast, say, to the unicorn, which only contingently proved to want for a bodily form beyond the discursive, or textual, *corpus*.

Although these considerations hardly exhaust the variety of ways in which objectivity and physical existence or being interweave, they are perhaps sufficient to make unmistakable the point made in our earlier chapters to the effect that the contrast between objective and physical being in what we experience is a fundamental contrast between two orders or frameworks that are not identical at every point, even when they happen to coincide. The objective and the physical depend upon one another without being coextensive and without being articulated in the same way. This last point is extremely important to take fully into account. The structure of experience and the structure of nature are, because of it, relatively independent variables.

We thus have a general rule: physical being, while it reveals itself within experience as involving a dimension that exceeds experience, also reveals itself on the material side as providing for experience a necessary lining. That is, experience, without being reducible to the points where physical and objective being are coincident, consists formally in an objective structure embodied through a lattice of physical relations that would not be just what they are apart from experience, but that are not the whole of experience either. The objective world (the world of experience) at once enfolds in part and restructures in part the physical environment within which it sustains itself. This is also true of the biosemiotic network of objective worlds taken as a totality (cf. Bargatzky 1978; Lovelock 1972, 1979, 1988).

We see thus that the action proper to signs is at the heart of the interplay between objective and physical being that constitutes experience, and illustrates in the constituting that the sign must be, as we saw in chapter 4, a purely relational being in order to function and act as it does in playing precisely this mediating role, beyond the dynamics of physical interaction (whether material and physical or psychological and psychic, as Peirce c.1906: 5.484 joined Poinsot 1632a: 195/3–9, 18–29 in pointing out). The sign manifests itself in semiosis not at all as a physical thing, nor even as a peculiar type and variety of object. The sign appears, rather, as the linkage whereby the objects, be they bodily entities or purely objective, come to stand one for another within some particular context or web of experience.

The semiotic web, it turns out, embraces not just the living world (the biosphere) nor even just the realm of cognizing organisms. The so-called physical world itself exists within the world of experience. But it is not *as* experienced that the physical world is properly called physical. As experienced, as we have seen, it is properly called *objective*. The *further* discrimination among objects of experience, between those that are *also* physical existents and those that are *only* objects of experience, is itself a matter of experience. The engrained dichotomy between the subjective on the one hand, which is all that is essentially private or illusory, and the objective on the other hand, which is what is public, real, and independent of the observer, simply fails to hold up when duly weighed and considered in the light of the only instrument we have for discriminating the true (or more sound) from the false (or less sound). A trichotomy is necessary, and a trichotomy of a most peculiar kind.

The essential category for the experienced as such is the category of the objective: whatever exists in any way as known. Opposed to the objective in this sense is both the physical in the sense of the things of the environment prejacent to and able as such to survive the demise of experience, and the subjective in the sense of the psychological or psychic depths of the individual insofar as they are not available objectively here and now. In other words, we have a trichotomy where the subject stands at the center of a web of relationships comprising precisely an objective world. Through the web, each subject is also entangled in other webs with other centers, the whole comprising an objective network. The filaments and strands of this network of intersecting webs catch aspects of subjectivities that exist through their bodily dimension as elements active in the physical environment below and beyond the ways in which the subject experiences that environment and reconstitutes it structurally as an objective world shareable with some others. The strands of this network then hold these aspects up for scrutiny from the centered perspectives and thereby objectivize the subjective aspects and incorporate them as aspects now of something else besides, namely, an Umwelt, a shared objective world, in its contrast to environment.

B. Species-Specific Objective Worlds

With this understanding of objectivity in mind, a useful concept for discussing the being of signs as constructive through experience of a world precisely objective throughout is that of the *Umwelt*. Originally formulated at the end of the nineteenth century by the biological researcher Jakob von Uexküll and developed through further researches well into this century (von Uexküll 1899–1940), this concept, with important modifications of its originally overly-Kantian and needlessly anti-evolutionary context of formulation, is commonly used in semiotics today in connection with the doctrine of signs.

The environment selectively reconstituted and organized according to the specific needs and interests of the individual organism constitutes an Umwelt. The Umwelt thus depends upon and corresponds to an *Innenwelt*, or cognitive map, developed within each individual. The Innenwelt enables the individual to find its way in the environment and insert itself into a network of communication, interest, and livelihood shareable especially with the several other individuals of its own kind. If the organism could not objectify enough of the physical surroundings to catch its food, for example, it would not, as Jacob more or less picturesquely remarked (1982: 56), live to tell the tale.

Of course, the possibility of coincidence of environmental with objective elements actually realized within experience and indefinitely expandable through the critical control of objectification lies at the heart of science and constitutes the basis and ground for all studies and experimentation properly termed scientific. But this possibility as critically verifiable is already owing to a special feature—textuality, as we shall see—whereby the specifically human Umwelt, the Lebenswelt, as it is times called, is a uniquely malleable Umwelt open in ways no other Umwelt on this planet is open to reconstitution along alternative lines of objectification, both within itself and in its relations with the external environment physical as such.

The Umwelt in principle, thus, is a "model world" from the point of view of possibility: it is one of the infinite variety of possible alternatives according to which the bare physical furnishings of the environment can be arranged and incorporated into an architectural superstructure of possible experiences, supposing especially this or that biological form. But from the point of view of its inhabitants, an Umwelt is the actual world of experience and everyday reality. In comparison to this actual world of experience, the prejacent physical in its proper being is secondary, derivative, and not necessarily recognized according to the intrinsic requirements of its own being.

We think today, for example, generally, that a human Umwelt incorporating the institution of slavery is a less acceptable species-specific habitat than one that is free of slavery. The "model world" of the twentieth century is sharply different in this regard from the "model world" acceptable to and inhabited by the ancient Greeks, Saint Paul, medieval man, and so forth. The Umwelt of Sparta differed sharply from that of Athens, and much appropriation of physical resources within the shared environment was put to the use of determining which objective model should dominate over or even supplant the other. Rome sought to destroy not the physical lining of the Carthaginian Umwelt so much as the Umwelt itself as sustained by that lining.

The notion of reality and the notion of the Umwelt are, from the point of view of experience, inseparable. Yet what is distinctive about human experience in contrast to a purely perceptually structured consciousness is, quite precisely, the discoverability that Umwelt and environment (or physical surroundings) are yet not coextensive. From this bare suspicion of the understanding in its difference from sense arises the whole enterprise of science and technology, on the one hand, and morality as distinct from mores, on the other.

The problem of the action of signs in the context of our own experience, therefore, is, fundamentally, the problem of the common source of all Umwelts (the emergence of objectivity *in its difference realized* from the physical environment as such), and, formally, the problem of the emergence within objectivity of the *realization of its difference* from the physical surroundings. This latter realization, we shall see, is tantamount to the invention of language or—what comes to the same thing—the advent of textuality. There may be forms of semiosis already at work in physical nature itself anterior to the advent of anything living and continuing independent of it, to be sure. But only with the Umwelt do we encounter in its full actuality the first phenomenon of semiosis, the explicit realization of the function essential to the sign: 'referral' or *renvoi*, the word by which Jakobson, as Sebeok well put it (1984a: 66) "deftly captured and transfixed each and every sign process conforming to the classic formula, *aliquid stans pro aliquo*" (one thing standing for another).[21]

This point is among the most fundamental points to be made in regard to the sign: there is no object that does not depend *in its objectivity* on the simultaneous action of the sign as making present in experience something other than itself, something that it itself is not.

The further point concerning what is species-specific to experience in a human Umwelt is well-made through an observation of Maritain's (1957: 52–54): on the one hand, animals other than humans make use of signs, but they do not know that there are signs; on the other hand, the birth of language and the grasp of the relation of signification as such—as distinct from the sign vehicle, or sensible embodiment of the sign as ground of semiosis, as well as from the object signified—are the same. For "what defines language is not precisely the use of words, or even of conventional signs; it is the use of any sign whatsoever as involving the knowledge or awareness of the relation of signification".[22] In this relation as such

---

21. This is the formula Jakobson employs (1979) as providing "a retrospective glance over the development of semiotic". It is an excellent formula, capturing the essence of the late Latin formula ("id quod repraesentat aliud a se potentiae cognoscenti") rejecting the ancient Stoic and Augustinian linkage of the sign to a sensible content as its vehicle ("signum est quod praeter species quas ingerit sensui, aliud facit in cognitionem venire"), on the one hand, and, on the other hand, capturing too the essential openness of semiosis to non-cognitive virtualities.

22. A semiotic approach to language pursued along this line, thus, would support Peirce's contention (c.1902a: 1.250) that "the question of the origin of language" is one "which must be settled before linguistics takes its final form", as against the Linguistic Society of Paris which adopted as the second article of its founding *Statuts* (1868: 3) that no communication concerning the origin of language be admitted into discussions of linguistic science.

consists formally and strictly, as distinct from fundamentally and perceptually, the *sign* in its proper being: "and therefore a potential infinity"—what later authors have called 'unlimited semiosis'; "it is the use of signs in so far as it manifests that the mind has grasped and brought out the relation of signification".

This feat opens the possibility of a text and establishes therewith the boundary beyond which zoösemiosis becomes specifically anthroposemiotic. At this moment the specifically closed Umwelt is opened up to the prospect of infinity; zoösemiosis becomes anthroposemiosis, capable of a progression into infinity.[23]

C. SPECIES-SPECIFICALLY HUMAN SEMIOSIS

Once the relation of signification has been grasped on its own, as distinct from a particular object signifying another particular object signified, it becomes possible to detach that relation from any particular objective sign vehicle and, taking this invisible content itself as the basis for further representations, to attach it, instead, to some other object. This other object will now serve, by choice, in lieu of the original vessel—that is, will now serve as ground for a relation originally grounded elsewhere. With the possibility of such a choice, a new kind of sign and a new mode of signifying comes into existence objectively, the *stipulable* sign.

What we call "linguistic signs" are a specific variety or sub-species of the stipulable sign. The members of this sub-specific set are arbitrary in their ground over-all, although natural inasmuch as they consist in relationships no less than (and precisely as do) other kinds of signs as such—for example: signs embodying connections that are physical before becoming also objective and social (such as the connections between clouds and rain or smoke and fire); or signs formed of connections that are objective associatively rather than physically (such as the connections between candlelight and lovers, napkins and meals); or of connections that are manipulative (such as pressing a lever and receiving a pel-

---

23. Sebeok (1989b: 83), resuming in effect an ancient controversy of the greatest interest for the doctrine of signs (cf. Poinsot 1632a: Second Preamble, esp. 102/23–25 and 102/36–105/13; Appendix C, esp. 380/23–381/40), observes, presumably against an idealist formulation that has become current in the wrong ways among semiotic *literati*, that "semiosis is by no means unlimited (save perhaps in a metaphysical sense)." But what cannot happen in a semiosis either virtual or simply exercised is precisely what happens in a semiosis signified in its very actuality–that is to say, in the making of a text: relations as such are made to found other relations (and, of course, there is nothing to prevent the physicist in particular, thanks to the anthroposemiosis through which physics and the mathematics on which it depends modally exist, from hypothecating and consequently asserting the opposite).

It is thus that semiotics explains infinite generability in the sphere of anthroposemiosis and of sentences within language in particular, without having to postulate (Chomsky 1968) a separate "faculty of language", distinct from intelligence.

let of food) rather than stipulative; or social signs subsequent to language embodying connections which are only objective and cultural (such as the connection between flag and country). The ability to grasp the actual stipulation of linguistic signs, in contrast to making associations based on their perceptible aspects, is just what is meant by "intelligence" in the species-specific sense of linguistic competence.[24] This ability is "a subspecies of semiotic competence", as Johansen says (1985: 279), which overlays the biological species-specific competence with a developmental dimension historical in a Lamarckian sense, thus introducing into the objective world of the species the permeating element of textuality.

Using the older terminology of images and ideas along with conceptual premises that are pre-zoösemiotic, Maritain attempted thus to describe the situation (1957: 53):

> Normally in the development of a child it is necessary that the idea be "enacted" by the senses and lived through before it is born as an idea; it is necessary that the relationship of signification should first be actively *exercised* in a gesture, a cry, in a sensory sign bound up with the desire that is to be expressed. *Knowing* this relationship of signification will come later, and this will be to have the *idea*, even if it is merely implicit, of that which is signified. Animals and children make use of this signification; they do not perceive it. When the child begins to perceive it (then exploits it, toys with it, even in the absence of the real need to which it corresponds)—at that moment the idea has emerged.

But this description fails in its purpose, unless it is *further* made clear that the detachment of the relationship from the related elements is achieved in such a way that the relation in its proper being as imperceptible can be made an objective foundation or basis that, directly as such (that is, *as* imperceptible), is able *further* to serve to stand for and represent some other relationship yet again. (Whether that other relationship terminate at an object that is *also* imperceptible in turn is not what matters, although it does emphasize what is distinctive to the semiosis in question). A dog, for example, wanting to be let out, can indeed learn to fake the need to evacuate as a way of manipulating its master "even in the absence of the real need to which it corresponds". And yet, at that

---

24. This is also the meaning of "intelligent life" in the sense of what radio astronomers earnestly search for among the physical stimuli rendered objective by their remarkable (if no doubt remarkably primitive) instruments. It is improbable that such a lifeworld—a radically flexible and open *Lebenswelt* such as Husserl showed at the base of the sciences and the humanities, in contrast with the *Umwelten* at best partially flexible and finally encapsulated wholes of other species—has evolved only once and at one place in the physical totality of the prejacent surroundings. Be that as it may, it is from within the Umwelt of such a species, a species able to mark for subsequent contemplation physically objective protrusions into its sphere, that the understanding of the sign, in contrast to its bare use, begins.

moment, an idea in the sense in question has not emerged, no matter how playful the dog may become in its efforts.

At the heart of the difference between the human Umwelt and the Umwelt of other cognitive organisms is the "idea" in this specifically semiotic sense: the relationship itself that constitutes signification is grasped in its proper being at once imperceptible and distinguishable both from a given signified and from a given sign-vehicle—and therefore as detachable from any given vehicle and attachable to any other vehicle, as well as directable to some other object, or to the same object only, in its new attachment. This difference makes for the possibility of a text as such.

Texts are not only literary. They can be any physical structure at all made to embody ideas in the semiotic sense. Indeed, the whole of culture, in this radical sense (cf. Danow 1987), is a text. In this sense, culture as a text is a network of signs whose lattice of articulations is chosen at critical nodes, though not at all nodes (which would be impossible, an outer limit of the intelligible, pushed, for example, in Joyce's *Finnegans Wake*). These critical nodes are chosen differently and to different degrees in individual cases but are also, as chosen, subsequently detached in effect from the initial choices and *naturalized* through the habit-patterns of a community as "conventions" in the strong sense of "the way we do things (by preference unthinkingly) here".

The network exhibits a hierarchical or quasi-hierarchical structure relative to the physical side of the objects experienced within the network's frame.[25] Thus, a technological artifact embodies critically controlled

---

25. Hjelmslev's remarks à propos of naive realism pertain here (1961: 22–23): "Naive realism would probably suppose that analysis consisted merely in dividing a given object into parts, i.e., into other objects, then those again into parts, i.e., into still other objects, and so on. But even naive realism would be faced with the choice between several possible ways of dividing. It soon becomes apparent that the important thing is not the division of an object into parts, but the conduct of the analysis so that it conforms to the mutual dependences between these parts, and permits us to give an adequate account of them. In this way alone the analysis becomes adequate and, from the point of view of a metaphysical theory of knowledge, can be said to reflect the 'nature' of the object and its parts.

"When we draw the full consequences from this, we reach a conclusion which is most important for an understanding of the principle of analysis: both the object under examination and its parts have existence only by virtue of these dependences; the whole of the object under examination can be defined only by their sum total; and each of its parts can be defined only by the dependences joining it to the other coordinated parts, to the whole, and to its parts of the next degree, and by the sum of the dependences that these parts of the next degree contract with each other. After we have recognized this, the 'objects' of naive realism are, from our point of view, nothing but intersections of bundles of such dependences. That is to say, objects can be described only with their help and can be defined and grasped scientifically only in this way. The dependences, which naive realism regards as secondary, presupposing the objects, become from this point of view primary, presupposed by their intersections."

Poinsot (1632: 270/39–43, and elsewhere passim), applying a formula from Cajetan 1507, established within his semiotic the ground for Hjelmslev's point: "The differences of things *as things* are quite other than the differences of things *as objects* and in the being of object;

and stipulated relativities no less than does an artistic or literary creation, and all three would serve as documentary evidence to some future historian or anthropologist or to an extraterrestrial seeking to understand the contemporary human Umwelt. But, whereas the objective relations embodied in the technological device *directly* relate *also* to its physical constitution *as such* in order for it to function as an instrument, the objective relations embodied in an artistic structure dominate the physical constitution of the whole in quite another fashion. Finally, the objective relations constitutive of the literary work tend to be a variable relatively free in respect to their embodiment, that is, their sensorially accessible base. For this reason the written word tends to function as the primary analogate for our understanding of text, inasmuch as here the relation of signification is exhibited not only as subject to critical control (that is, as cultural) but also in the form most subject to critical control (that is, the linguistic form) while still retaining permanence in the exhibition (the written in contrast to the spoken word).

To create a text is therefore to become aware of the difference between physical surroundings and objective world and to play with this difference, thereby erecting a system of signs at once expressly in consciousness of the difference and enhancive of it. To create a text is predicated on the understanding that "the role of the object in the semiosis is", as Johansen puts it (1985: 235), "not confined to being an element in an experiential situation interpreted to tell if a symbol applies or not". To create a text is hence to proceed accordingly in the use of signs freely to structure objectivity in a contour and manner accessible only to a conspecific, in the precise sense of another organism able to share that understanding and to grasp signs fashioned on its basis (that is to say, encoded according to patterns neither reducible to nor accessible within the perceptible dimension as such of the sign structure). To create a text is thus a function of musement.

For an understanding of this function two terms must be clarified: code and idea.

D. The "Conventionality" of Signs in Anthroposemiosis

When the term "ideas" is defined semiotically, that is, as the individual discovery of relation as such as the connection and difference between sign and signified, the question becomes: how is such a discovery shared? How is a relation of signification grasped for itself as detachable from this sign-vehicle and attachable rather to that one, communicated

---

and things that differ in kind or more than in kind in the one line can differ in the other line not at all or not in the same way."

in its difference? That is the question to which the term "code" is proposed as answer. In other words, "idea" is to Innenwelt as code is to Umwelt as species-specifically (and regardless of planetary location) human. To understand what a text is and to understand the human lifeworld in what is specific to it are the same.

The perceptions of an animal that learns through experience, and the beliefs of a human animal as subject to rational criticism, are keys to textuality as the species-specific human form of objectivity. We distinguish among "fancies" the two distinct iconic forms: images, derivable from and reducible to a correlation between objects sensorially accessible as such (given a specific biological endowment), and conceptions or ideas, which express relations of signification in the being proper to them as relations (that is, as indifferent to their subjective ground and, consequently, as detachable from any given sign-vehicle as object for attachment to an objective ground elsewhere and otherwise). Ideas in this sense, conceptions within perceptions of the world, are unique to, and species-specifically definitive of, anthroposemiosis.

But in order to establish the basis for *shared* conceptions, these ideas must be embodied in a publicly accessible objective structure, which is not the case as long as their only embodiment is the cerebral cortex of the individual for whom a given idea has taken form. A given objective relation, seen in its detachability, must not only be detached but also attached elsewhere: it must be *assigned* a new ground in such a way that that new ground can in turn be experienced as a sign-vehicle relative to the objectivity originally grasped elsewhere. The code is the correlation and proportioning of a sensibly accessible element to an objectivity that is understood as correlated thereto. The idea must be correlated with some physical element within experience that is taken to serve as ground for the relation in which the idea expressly consists. That correlation is what constitutes a *code* in its difference from an idea.

Code and idea alike are logical interpretants,[26] but the logical interpretant considered now on the side of Innenwelt (idea), now on the side of Umwelt (code). A code thus channels and directs relations among objects in a publicly accessible way. A mastery of the encoding will result in a partial duplication (a sufficient overlap, we might say) within the decoder of the ideas behind the original encoding, thereby imposing, to that extent, a *common conception* (an *intersubjective moment*) within and beyond

---

26. An interpretant in general is the ground on which an object functions as a sign. Interpretants exist, consequently, at those points in semiosis where objects are transformed into signs or signs are transformed into other signs. Ideas are interpretants, but not all interpretants are ideas: interpretants as such are indifferently physical or even mental. They define the points of innovation in semiosis at the level of objective representation, as we explained in chapter 3 above. Logical interpretants define the points of innovation in intellectual semiosis, that is, developing understanding.

the perceptually shared objectivity. The Umwelt, in itself perceptual through and through according to the species-specific constraints of a biological inheritance, is now modified and restructured from within by further objective relations not themselves constrained directly by the biological heritage. Code, in short, belongs to the object experienced and idea to the organism experiencing. Both alike serve to ground, channel, and define or specify the relationships of dependency that comprise the objective world in its integral being subsumptive of the physical.

So far we have noted that semiosis, in the fullest sense of the action of signs, extends well beyond the boundaries of culture, as even well beyond the boundaries of animal societies, to include the dynamics of plant life and even the dynamics of chemistry and physics down to the quantum level insofar as there is a question of *future outcomes* and *law governed interaction*. Our concentration has been on the explicit absorption and redistribution of elements of physical environment within the relational network of objective world through cognitively mediated experience. We have focused on the construction of species-specific Umwelts corresponding to Innenwelts for the purpose of providing the proximate genus in contrast to which the specific difference of a human world—a Lebenswelt—might become visible.

That difference, we now see, is textuality, in the precise sense of the introduction, through understanding, of relations into the objective world that are not grounded in the perceptible elements, as such, of that Umwelt as correlated with a species-specific biological heritage. These relations alter the objectivity itself experienced and add to that experience the element of critical control as a possibility. Such control is not in the bare sense of something modified or modifiable through the muscular effort and plan of the organism (such as, for example, the beaver contemplating a mountain stream before and after building its dam), but in the rich sense of recognizing the possible, in its objective being, as distinct from the whole order of physical elements as such actually given here and now.

The exaptation[27] of the human modeling system (let us say, language in the ground sense) through speech into a communication system is therefore only one aspect of textuality: specifically, that aspect wherein the communicative intention finds an embodiment that is distinct from the other purposes that enter in when action is directed, beyond language, to the establishment of the postlinguistic structures of civil organization, shelter, trade, clothing, and so forth. These other systems, too,

---

27. This is the term introduced by Gould and Vrba (1982) to designate the secondary adaptation whereby an organ or function originally developed within evolution for one purpose is then put to another use entirely: in this case, human language, originally developed as a unique modeling system, is then further deployed through real relations to communicative purposes precisely according to what is unique about it.

depend on the stipulable sign actualized in a determinate way (a "conventional sign") in the fullest sense of an alternative contingent embodiment of the relation of signification grasped in itself, as distinct from any given subjective ground. But these other systems are required to take account of their material embodiment as objects created to perform more than a communicative function (in the case of a house, for example, to withstand the elements; in the case of a machine, to work reliably; and so on). In contrast, the language as exapted to communicate, through embodiment in a system of sense perceptible elements, needs to take no more account of the bodily form than is minimally necessary to the one function in its purity. For this function no more is needed than to convey the code, according to which the relations constituted by ideas have been transferred from the Innenwelt to the Umwelt, as determinative of the experience of others able to grasp the code precisely in its conventional being (its situation of being incidental to the sensible constitution of its immediate ground, its "arbitrariness" in happening to be this way from customs dimanated from stipulations). Thus, the animals other than humans perceive the difference between the general's uniform and that of the private, but only the human animals have a chance to understand the difference not in its material effects (for the animals, too, experience social power relations) but in its formal constitutive (which is first of all cultural and only derivatively social).

In this sense we can agree with Barthes that "every semiological system has its linguistic admixture" (1964: 10; cf. Culler 1982: 21). At the same time our point is more basic: *every linguistic system has its semiological surplus*. The language is not only not an autonomous system, still less "a semiotic into which all other semiotics may be translated" (Hjelmslev 1961: 109). The structural peculiarity of language is not unlimited in that sense. But language is unlimited in the sense of being able to draw all other semiotics (and semiosis) into the trajectory of the communicative intention freed from a species-specific *biological* inheritance. The "linguistic admixture", far from providing the foundation of all other semiotics, pertains rather to their surplus and perfection in community—that is to say, as they are drawn into and made shareable through the diaphanous medium and network of relations (the codes in particular) through which the objective world receives a texture of intelligence.

In such community, the contexts of nature itself and of biosemiosis in particular are enhanced and transformed according to objective possibilities not prefigured as such in or by the biological heritage of the species. These possibilities are opened up, rather, through the Lamarckian means of convention, which is transmissible through the praeterphysical vehicle of correlating codes embodied in physical elements reworked with understanding. Included in such transmissible convention are the physical elements of linguistic communication. These achieve a semiotic pre-eminence by virtue of being independent of any specific purpose, in order to be, in the context of communication, at the service of every other purpose. Language as a communication system—as a publicly available coding of the Umwelt—is thus the objective reflection of the freedom of the intellect as a growth in time.[28]

At the same time the coding of the Umwelt is not restricted or reducible to linguistic coding in this sense. According to our anthroposemiotic definition of ideas, the coding of the Umwelt is the series of marks made by intelligence on the objective world *in whatever respect and whether deliberately or as a concomitant attribute of intelligent action*. The conventionalizing of objective relations makes of the context of Umwelts and physical relations the one texture of human experience. This "conventionalizing", this "loosening up" of the objective world as naturally determined (by biological heredity on one side and physical environment on the other) whereby reality itself becomes in some measure "freely chosen" (in Powell's phrase, 1983), constitutes the network of *codes* in the broadest sense, including the linguistic code as a subset. This conventionalizing of objective relations is not something actual or actualizable in only one way. It is something multiply actual (the diversity of the natural languages) and only virtually universal.[29] Such a virtual universality is destined always to be defeated in time by the particular actualizations called into being by specific circumstances on this planet,

---

28. "The invasion of codes", Eco remarks (1977: 27), "means that we are not gods: we are moved by rules. But we ought to decide (and here the epistemologies of code are in disagreement) whether we are not gods because we are motivated on the basis of rules which historically we give ourselves, or if we are not gods because divinity is precisely the Rule (the Code of Codes) which stands behind us."

Eco sees the choice as between the historical and the mechanistic; but this seems to overstate the situation. The question is whether codes are not a finite mediating ground *between* nature and culture, wherein the "Code of Codes" is neither immutable nor wholly freely chosen from within culture. The choice, then, is not between a frame of reference either historical or mechanistic but between seeing culture as a semiotic phenomenon cut off from nature by linguistic coding or seeing culture as founded in while transforming at its own level—that is to say, through the semiotic modalities characteristic of anthroposemiosis—the "natural" Umwelt.

29. The situation is well described by Bakhtin (1963: 202): "For the word is not a material thing but rather the eternally mobile, eternally fickle medium of dialogic interaction. It never gravitates toward a single consciousness or a single voice. The life of the word is contained in its transfer from one mouth to another, from one context to another context, from one social collective to another, from one generation to another generation. In this process the word does not forget its own path and cannot completely free itself from the power of these concrete contexts into which it has entered.

"When a member of a speaking collective comes upon a word, it is not as a neutral word of language, not as a word free from the aspirations and evaluations of others, uninhabited by others' voices. No, he receives the word from another's voice and filled with that other voice. The word enters his context from another context, permeated with the interpretations of others. His own thought finds the word already inhabited. Therefore the orientation of a word among words, the varying perception of another's word and the various means for reacting to it, are perhaps the most fundamental problems for the metalinguistic study of any kind of discourse, including the artistic."

and most likely on planets elsewhere, as giving rise, through semiosis, to a biosphere and intelligent life in the sense that we are speaking of it here as anthroposemiotic. Yet between these particular realizations there yet always remains the virtuality whereby one system of coding *could be*, given sufficient ingenuity, *translated into* the other, so that the virtually universal also defeats the actual particular in its own way, though only potentially and in the background.

In such a context we can appropriate Eco's conclusion (1977: 52): "To see cultural life as a web of codes and as a continuous reference from code to code is to restore to the human animal its true nature"—as long as we realize that the "nature" we are restoring the human animal to is its nature as semiosic *in actu signato*. The human animal, as inventor of the Rule, needs also to realize that this inventor is in dire need of being wary of the surrounding virtualities which measure, in every case, how truly reasonable the "rule" is against the background and in the context of what humanity must depend on (such as the rain forests or the ozone layer, and biosemiosis in general) in order to pursue its seemingly (but not entirely in fact) "unlimited semiosis". Otherwise, we risk making a semiotics on the model of the Hobbesian King, answerable to nothing below and hence immune to considerations of justice or injustice.

The codes themselves of culture already incorporate through the content of what they are used to convey (their "surplus", semiologically speaking) what is more than culture and binds it to the further reality of surroundings as physical. This whole which is more than language and within which language functions as a relational dependency suspended between what it presupposes and what presupposes it is the primary reality of human experience as a whole. We move from the idea of reality as an order of existence independent of the observer to a semiotic idea of "reality" as including also the observer in all that is dependent on the observer, along with whatever in experience reveals itself as a part of something—the old idea of "reality"—independent of the observer ("physical being" in its praeter-objective character as the *lining* of experience). We move from the classical modern idea of reality, which was the

---

Barthes (1970) speaks similarly of code as "so many fragments of something that has always been *already* read, seen, done, experienced; the code is the wake of that *already*".

But the code is more than a wake of the past: it is at the same time a wave of the future as it is taken up, modified, and given life anew by the individual appropriating an old understanding or forging a new one within the Lebenswelt. The code provides not a prisonhouse (Jameson 1972) but a clearinghouse, wherein the most prominent item is not the past but the colorful "fact that words have a capacity for learning" (Johansen 1985: 240) and an orientation towards the future. Bakhtin (1963: 166) has a beautiful answer to Peirce's inquiry "whether meaning does not always refer to the future" (c.1902: 24): "Nothing conclusive has yet taken place in the world, the ultimate word of the world and about the world has not yet been spoken, the world is open and free, everything is still in the future and will always be in the future".

ancient and medieval idea as well (Deely 1984: 265–266), to the post-modern idea of reality as the text of specifically human experience. We move from communication in the service of biological ends to a communication system opening as well possible worlds beyond any species-specific objective one, or any imaginary reductionistic purely physical one (the myth of Positivism).

Such is the movement within objectivity from sign to textuality, that is to say, to an objectivity which includes within its network of objective relations a dimension or aspect, an "affordance", in Gibson's phrase (1979—though not his sense: see Cunningham 1988), whereby objectification itself can be subjected to critical control and reshaped by stipulation. This brings us to the matter of criticism. This is a method proper to *les sciences humaines*, indeed, but an activity no less essential to the evaluation of presentations in the natural sciences and, in general, the activity distinctive of anthroposemiosis in its linguistic and cultural development beyond animal societies and the communications proper to zoösemiosis.

E. CRITICISM AS THE EXPLORATION OF TEXTUALITY

We have seen that the codes demarcating culture in its proper being incorporate, while at the same time contrast with, the physical side of objects and the objective "things" comprising together the Umwelts (the experience and structures of experience) of the various species interacting within the objective human world or (outside our awareness perhaps—but vitally and biologically in contrast with "culturally") within the organismic population comprising the human species as a biological entity. We have also seen that such codes are only incompletely actualized (within consciousness especially), while remaining operative virtually as a totality at cross purposes with itself (in the residual oppositions of perspective encoded into the objective world through past discourse and social interaction). Hence, for example (Eco 1977: 31; cf. Carleton 1649: sec. 6): "From one speaker to another there can be differences in the complexity of semantic analysis of a term: these differences produce *sub-codes* on the basis of which one speaker could assign meanings to the terms which other speakers would not assign to them; the different mastery of such sub-codes reveals class differences in social interaction".

Consequently, criticism is not merely "literary". It is an activity of mind that ranges across the entire horizon of objectivity textualized, including those types of objectification characterizing natural science. There are as many authentic roles for criticism as there are ways of bringing into the objective sphere, with greater explicitness and formalizing, the roles played or playable by the traces left in experience of the workings of intelligence over these many generations present through the past. Such traces are especially apparent in the linguistic sign ("the ideological phenomenon par excellence", as Vološinov remarked [1929: 13]), but also in general in that surplus of semiosis we have come to call "textuality" or "culture" in the sense of postlinguistic structures (Deely 1982: 198 n. 1, after Morris 1946).

Given this purview, the semiological systems of Roland Barthes and Jacques Derrida find in spite of themselves a theoretical ground within what Sebeok calls (1977: 181) the "major tradition" of semiotic development. So also do the systems after Eco (1973: 153; 1976) that, without being called semiological by their proponents, yet share the ideology of equating semiosis with the tracings and workings of codes precisely as conventional (in the base sense of standing in part on that irreducible element of the arbitrary which is inseparable from even though not identical with the stipulability of signs) within culture, lucubrating (in consequence) absorption of the indexical and iconic as such.

This label, as we saw in chapter 1, is a reference to a strategy for encouraging a view of semiotics not as a *theory* in either the traditional critical sense or in the traditional scientific sense, but as what Locke called a *doctrine* of signs (1690: 361–362; commentary in Deely 1986a, 1986c), a term which must be carefully construed. In the context of Locke's *Essay*, as Sebeok first pointed out (1976a: ix), "doctrine" has a unique sense, one redolent in particular of the Latin Renaissance mainstream understanding of philosophical knowledge in its double contrast with empirically soluble formulations on one side and theological formulations dependent on religious authority on the other side (Deely 1982: 127–130, 1986b). A doctrine of signs, within this notion of philosophical doctrine generally, specifically transcends the opposition of culture to nature, and thereby precludes an autonomously linguistic or literary semiotics, pretensions toward which, as we have seen, Sebeok (1977) rightly dubbed collectively a "minor tradition" respecting semiotics as a whole.

Such a *doctrina signorum* was specifically inaugurated in Poinsot's work (1632a: 38/16–20, 117/28–118/6), though the fullness of its object was not stated before Peirce, who coined the name *semiosis* (c.1906: 5.488) for the action through which this relative being of signs so artfully disengaged and delineated by Poinsot is sustained and fulfilled through actions. Thus, the doctrine of signs has for its unifying object, as we saw in Chapter 3, the action of signs explicitly recognized as an activity or process constructive not only of human experience but of all organismic experience and, we shall argue, of the physical environment itself. The argument of the chapter following is that the environment in its physical being is already developmental, and therefore virtually semiosic, by virtue, that is, of its tending to give rise to and to subsequently support and lend itself to appropriate transformation by the plethora of Umwelts (including the species-specifically human one) precisely in their contrast— as objective worlds—to the physical realm they presuppose. The objective worlds not only rest upon this prejacent physicality, they subsume it in part as it is in its own right, even while restructuring it directly in the objective order as well as subjectively through physical interactions as subjects.

The decisive move in this strategy for establishing the doctrine of signs on the basis of its full and proper possibilities for understanding today turns, not surprisingly, on our conception of *language*. We saw above, in line with our view of language as (prior to exaptation) the species-specifically human Innenwelt, that the essence of language is arguably equatable with the discovery of the relation of signification and the consequent reconstitution of experienced signs as stipulatable. This latter point refers to the subsequent use of any sign in the light of an apprehended difference between, on the one hand, an object signified as such, and, on the other hand, a sign-vehicle (or *signifier*) as such, in their mutual difference from the *linkage itself between* the two as able to be abstracted and codified for purposes of communication. By the same stroke, we saw, a field of infinite possibilities opened up—the field of unlimited semiosis. As Merrell briefly put it (1988: 257): "if a dog and the idea of a dog were separate, then there would be a relation between them, and therefore an idea of this relation, and so on, *ad infinitum*."

In giving a place to textuality as the objectivity proper to human beings, we see that what is required at the foundation is a notion of language larger and more fundamental than the network of differences conveyed through the employment of the arbitrary array we call (in relation to the network of conventions and contrasts constituting them formally) "linguistic signs". Maritain observes of this larger notion, this surplus creating the admixture whereby the whole of culture is textualized (1964: 91):

The term *language* does not relate only to the words which we use, it covers also all that which serves us to make ourselves understood, and therefore the whole imagery which we use and which is that of the persons to whom we speak, at such and such a moment of time and in such and such a place on earth. (Supposing that through some telephone through duration we could tell a contemporary of Julius Caesar something which concerns our epoch, could we speak to him of airplanes and of electronic machines, of the British Parliament, or of the Presidium of the Communist Party? The other person would not understand anything; it would indeed be necessary to use the imagery furnished by his own type of culture, as well as his own words and his own syntax.)

Given the coextensiveness, then, of textuality with the objective world of human experience (of a Lebenswelt in contrast to a pure Umwelt, let us say), the question becomes one of how to construe the "linguistic admixture" demonstrable within every semiological system—that is, within the totality of human experience, including the experience of "nature" so-called. This question brings us to the heart of the matter of what semiotics finally is, and what it has to contribute to the study of either branch or any subdivision of the accepted division of university studies today into the "sciences" on the one hand and the "humanities" on the other, including literature.

F. A Matrix for All the Sciences

The main point in this regard is that semiotics pertains to a renewal of the foundations of our understanding of knowledge and experience across the board, and hence to a transformation of the disciplinary superstructures culturally distributing that understanding (the traditional disciplines as currently founded). Semiotics also pertains to the renewal of any single currently established discipline within, say, the humanities, but only by way of achieving a proper understanding of semiosis itself in some particular. It is thus not just a question of putting aside the ill-advised or, as Culler more mordantly muses (1981: 20), "futile attempt to distinguish the humanities from the social sciences". It is, rather, a question of new foundations for the "sciences" in the ancient sense of the whole panoply of disciplinarily diversified human knowledge—be the object of the diversity "human", "natural", or "social" (in the current description). Semiotics is a perspective concerned with the matrix of all the disciplines, precisely as they are offsprings within experience of anthroposemiosis.

This claim is at the heart of semiotics' so-called "imperialism". It is not a question of imperialism, however, but of recognizing the role of experience as the ground of understanding throughout and the centrality of history in making of that ground a rich soil. It is more a question of *recovering from* the imperialism of the natural sciences, physics in particular, as the distinct heritage of positivism, and of seeing the subsets of semiosis within anthroposemiosis for what they are in relation to the whole.

Floyd Merrell makes the point nicely, in a note on his recent text (1988: 262 n. 12):

. . . in general the hermeneutical movement has been beneficial insofar as it has directed attention to the role of interpretation and understanding in the humanities. However, Stephen Toulmin observes, and rightly so [1982: 99–100], that this movement 'has done us a disservice' also because it does not recognize any comparable role for interpretation in the natural sciences and in this way sharply separates the two fields of scholarship and experience. Consequently, ... the central truths and virtues of hermeneutics have become encumbered with a whole string of false inferences and misleading dichotomies.

A truly "radical hermeneutics", such as Caputo calls for (1987), must first of all come round to the semiotic point of view, for that point of view, that standpoint, achieved its first systematic expression precisely by an author (Poinsot 1632: 38/1ff., commentary in Deely 1985, 1988) realizing and thematizing the point that interpretive activity or "hermeneutics" (the privileged term for the notion then was "perihermenias", as noted in Deely 1982: 188n.16) is coextensive with the life of the mind—and, we would add today, extensive of nature itself as engendering life.

This is the governing insight of the semiotic enterprise integrally conceived in all its phases and periods. Semiotics provides a perspective on the whole of experience in what is proper to it as experience. In achieving this, it becomes "first" among the sciences not as one among the others, such as traditional metaphysics envisaged, but as *doctrina* contrasts to *scientia* (Williams 1985; Anderson et al. 1984; Sebeok 1976a: ix) and as what is first in the understanding contrasts with what is derivative therefrom (Deely 1987, 1988, 1988a).

It is thus a question of realizing what is proper to the semiotic point of view, and of distinguishing what is foundational from what is consequent thereto and partial thereof. From the beginning, both from outside (for example, Ricoeur 1981 and after) and from within (for example, Bakhtin 1971,[30] Culler 1977), the semiotics movement has suffered from practitioners who mistook some part of semiosis for the whole of semiotics and who systematically strove to reduce the perspective of semiotic to the perspective of that preferred part with which they identified it. From within, the problem has been more serious, in that the European influence after Saussure, only now beginning to be absorbed and meliorated in the broader American influence emanating from Peirce, has cre-

---

30. The most startling example of mistaking semiotics from within is provided by the late notes of Bakhtin, who seems never to have recovered from his youthful conception of semiotics as of a piece with Russian Formalism (Bakhtin 1970–1971: 147): "Semiotics deals primarily with the transmission of ready-made communication using a ready-made code. But in live speech, strictly speaking, communication is first created in the process of transmission, and there is, in essence, no code".

This conclusion, especially to scholars steeped in Bakhtin, is inscrutable. I interpret "there is, in essence, no code" to say that "prejacent to and independent of the anthroposemiosis itself there is no actual code". This is suggested to me by the fact that the fragment containing the quotation in question ends abruptly in the middle of a tantalizing sentence, posing "The problem of changing the code in inner speech . . .". This, however, is only a guess.

What seems clear to me is that, in setting his own work (unmistakably and centrally semiotic in our terms) over against semiotics as he does, Bakhtin himself illustrates the prevalence as well as the seriousness of the misunderstanding behind the *pars pro toto* fallacy whereby a linguistic or literary semiotics comes to fancy itself as autonomous.

ated in the popular consciousness a de facto equation of semiotics with structuralist and literary concerns. To this day, in much of the literature sociologically defining the contemporary development of semiotics, a naive assumption remains transparently at work equating the semiotic point of view with literary preoccupations and tending toward the explicit extreme of equating semiosis with "the product of encoding signs" (Morgan 1985: 8). Thus, as prominent an author as Robert Scholes is able to assert (1982: ix) that, "usually defined as the study of signs (from a Greek root meaning *sign*), semiotics has in fact become the study of codes."

To all such views (the gamut of writings more or less dominated by the tendency within semiotics toward this explicit extreme) apply Sebeok's blunt rejoinder (1984b: 2) to Hawkes (1977: 124): "Nothing could be a more deluded misconstrual of the facts of the matter, but the speciousness of this and associated historical deformations are due to our own inertia in having hitherto neglected the serious exploration of our true lineage".

What is fundamentally misguided about the semiological tendency to treat intertextuality as a self-contained whole, centered on the literary sign and closed in upon itself through an unlimited (but autistic) semiosis, is the compartmentalization of culture from nature by the inappropriate importing of the presuppositions of idealistic philosophy into the perspective opened by the sign. The perspective opened by the sign is as removed from idealism as it is from realism in the requirements proper to its own development. The study of sign action cannot properly be confined to the boundaries of the artifactual nor measured by the paradigm of linguistic exchanges. If such study is artificially so confined and measured, it is cut off from the context required ultimately even for the intelligibility of the literary, as Johansen demonstrates in his "Prolegomena to a semiotic theory of text interpretation" (1985).

If, while striving to be semiotic, a perspective takes for its object specifically literary textuality as constituted terminatively, that is, as itself objectified and scrutinized as known—much as if it were the "given" for semiotics comparable to the stones of the geologist or the reptilian bones of paleontology—such a perspective has yet to achieve the standpoint proper to the sign. The perspective proper to semiotics arises rather, exactly as in Locke's anomalous conclusion (1690: 361–362), with the idea of the idea as a nexus of relationships that carry the cognizant subject beyond itself and constitute at the same time, on the basis of a cognitive map of the environment, an Umwelt, which is strictly irreducible to the prejacent physical and species-specific for every life form, including the human one. This human Umwelt or "Lebenswelt", as we have seen, in contrast to the *Umwelten* of purely zoösemiotic life forms, has a unique texture through which it is transformable into an asymptotic number of variant models, through the unique *moyen* of language.

In the end, the idea of reality as the species-specific objective world is what gives intelligibility and place to the activity of all criticism, whether it aims at developing one side of the contrast between the environmentally given and the specifically constructed, as in literary criticism, or at distinguishing the specifically constructed in order to concentrate on the environmentally given, as in much scientific criticism. The relationship of Innenwelt to Umwelt is such that we finally understand that what has been called "fiction", for example, is not an imitation of something else so much as an expression of a semiosis that makes of the something else just as easily an imitation of what began as fiction (see Toews' analysis of contemporary historians in terms of 'William of Baskerville' in Williams and Pencak 1991). In this way, as Culler puts it (1981: 38), "one of the effects of semiotics is to question the distinction between literary and nonliterary discourse".

It is a question of remodeling the world—the objective world—but as this objective world includes in its proper being something also of physical surroundings. The question is not so much simply that "realism is in essence deeply mythic" (Con Davis 1985: 56) as that reality—the reality of human experience, wherein the line between what is dependent upon and independent of interpretive activity can never be finally drawn because that very line itself shifts with each new achievement of understanding—is in essence thoroughly semiosic.

Literature, as the most presuppositioned and purely objective phase of anthroposemiosis (able to deal directly with the object as nonexistent instead of having to discover its nonexistence by chagrin, as sometimes happens in natural science or in history), requires the most complete account of signification. While a literary "text itself need not refer to any past experiences", nonetheless, "experience of objects, actions, or events, similar to what is referred to in a given text, is a prerequisite to the understanding of it" (Johansen 1985: 261–262; cf. King 1987).

G. A Model for Discourse as Semiosis

That and how the universe of discourse—any discourse, including literary—"is bound up with the experience of the parties" to the discourse is what the literary scholar Dines Johansen has shown in an essay expressly regarding the problem of situating literature and literary criticism within the more general purview of semiosis as it is regarded in the major tradition of contemporary semiotic development. We can usefully introduce Johansen's model for anthroposemiosis (1982: 473, 1985:

266), as including specifically the literary. The model is here editorially modified, mainly by enhancing by explicitly labeling the identification of the ten axes defining the planes constitutive of "the semiotic pyramid". Johansen's reasons for introducing this model are also our own (1985: 265): on the one hand, it is intended as a heuristic device which should make it possible to recognize the multiple relationships of each element; on the other hand, it should further the inquiry into the nature of the signifying process by calling attention to the interrelations between certain aspects of meaning production and interpretation, and, of course, by provoking objections:

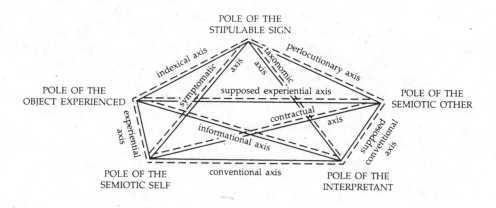

FIGURE 2. *The Pyramid of Anthroposemiosis*

For purposes of making explicit critical possibilities afforded by this model for approaching explication of texts of whatever objective type, we might here fruitfully redistribute the pyramid according to the ten interdependent triangular planes comprising the model—six radiating from the sign-pole, four from the organismic poles of interpreter and utterer—in order to underscore how presuppositioned and farthest removed from autonomy ("the myth of intertextuality and intersemioticity", as we might say) a literary semiotics is in the scheme of experience. In effect, Johansen's pyramid can be made to serve as an interpretant for Bakhtin's remark (1975: 48) that the language of a novel "is a system of intersecting planes" which, moreover, bind it to common experiences underlying scientific texts as well (Figure 3).

If one enters seriously into Johansen's argument that the semiotics of texts, when pursued integrally rather than according to faddish abstractions, involves one with all these planes simultaneously (but according to emphases that, of course, can be varied for the purposes of the

1. Proposition Plane

2. Communication Plane

3. Convention Plane

4. Representation Plane

5. Supposed Convention Plane

6. Supposed Representation Plane

7. Interactional Plane

8. Intersignificational Plane

9. Utterer's Informational Plane

10. Interpreter's Informational Plane

FIGURE 3. *The Planes of Semiosis within Discourse*

analysis at hand), one also begins to see how a literary semiotics might be constituted in the full scope of the possibilities afforded to it by the doctrine of signs.

These possibilities are made visible precisely when the foundational inquiries of the doctrine of signs are made commensurate with the full scope of semiosis, as a process subtending the whole of nature so far as nature involves a development in time along lines that transcend the physically established patterns of any given moment in the cosmic evolution. As that framework makes itself visible in the diverse works contributing more and more consciously to its edification, we see that the "place marked out in advance" for semiotics and giving it "a right to existence", in Saussure's curious expression (i.1906–1911: 33; cf. Russell 1982), is something that cannot be defined in a way exclusive of any activity of interpretation but rather can be defined only inclusive thereof.

To study the sign is to uncover semiosis, and therewith a web as vast as nature itself. The arrangement, the web of renvoi sustaining the environmental and sensible elements at each moment according to patterns that are not themselves sensible nor reducible to what is sensible, constitutes the semiotic object in its full possibilities for understanding.

This is a "reality" quite different from that prejacent given in which the mind had no part and to which the observer contributed hopefully nothing, conceived by the medievals and sought by the moderns. Nor is it a reality wholly reducible to the mind's own workings on the basis of a hidden outer realm and a hidden inner mechanism of understanding linked only by the phenomena constituted by the mind itself, as Kant concluded. Something much richer than either reduction, something more collusive even than the rapport between fly trap and fly in the realm of insects and flowers, this newer paradigm—in a phrase, semiotic reality—recognizes that the boundary between what is dependent upon and what is independent of interpretive activity can never be finally fixed from within experience because the boundary itself fluctuates in function of the development of understanding, whether "speculative" or "practical", "scientific" or "literary".

Like the human sciences themselves, "semiotics is not only a field of different approaches to a unique object but also a field of sometimes conflicting philosophical definitions of this unique object" (Eco 1979: 77). Furthermore (and in this it provides the matrix for natural science as well), semiotics is the field studying the process whereby any object is constituted in its full actuality as known: not simply as a process in nature, but also as the *prise de conscience* whereby nature becomes fully aware of itself and achieves its final totality in the transcendence over physical being. This process of transcendence begins with the historical Umwelten and is fully realized in the reflexivity of the Lebenswelt that makes of each text a prospective intertext incorporating life and fiction and the whole of nature as well through a semiosis metaphysically unlimited— and even physically, though limited, not wholly determinately so. This situation has been personified by Floyd Merrell (1988: 260) in a creature far more worthy of the talents of Disney artists than the pedestrian Roger Rabbit. Imagine a filmic rendering of *the Chimerical Octopus*, constructed on the following plan:

> Consider each sign possibility to be a point . . . with an infinite set of lines connecting it to all other points in the universe. . . . Each sign-point is like a chimerical octopus whose body is the point and whose tentacles are the infinite number of lines emanating from that point ready to suck in one or more of all the other sign-points, which then become its interpretant and hence another sign-point. (Actually, more in accord with Laplace and God, each tentacle would have an eye at its extremity enabling it to 'see' all other sign-points simultaneously.)
>
> This entire conglomeration of lines, to be true to form, will have certain characteristics: (a) the whole can be 'cut' at any point and re-connected along any one of its lines, like Peirce's amorphous 'book of assertions' [1903: 4.512]; (b) at a given instant the conglomerate is static (the synchronic dimension), but it holds the possibility for all future connections (the diachronic dimension)—this instant is not the Saussurean slice out of the semiological salami, it is the entire conglomerate given 'en bloc', holding all past, present, and future possibilities; and (c) the conglomerate is self-contained, twisting and doubling back on itself, like Einsteinian space-time (called the "block" universe), or like an infinity of infinitely thin Möbius strips intersecting each other at the point of their twist. However, (d) with respect to finite sign users, unlike point-octopuses, all observations and relations must remain inside: there is no global vision, for immanence rules—commensurate with quantum theory, which has demolished the classical view of subject/object and observer/observed. And (e) there can be no complete description of the whole since, commensurate with Peirce's plastic 'book of assertions', logical connections do not remain the same over time, and since, with our own finite number of appendages and sensory organs, we can never process all signs in an instant.

H. SUMMATION

Among the human sciences, semiotics is unique in being a study concerned with the matrix of all the sciences, and in revealing the centrality of history to the enterprise of understanding in its totality. The centrality of history to understanding is revealed through the codes of culture that alone sustain, beyond the individual insight, the *commens* (Peirce 1906: 196–197) or shared mentality that defines a language (such as English), a discipline (such as physics or literary criticism), a subculture (such as the Gays), a nation (such as Israel), and, ultimately, civilization itself in all its conflicting strands of historically embedded interpretations giving structure to the everyday experience of the conspecifics capable of language. We can thus say, in view of the larger sense of language sketched by Maritain and insisted upon independently by Bakhtin

(1971: 214, as cited in Todorov 1981: 56): "in living speech, messages are, strictly speaking, created for the first time in the process of transmission, and ultimately" (that is, prejacent to, and independent of, the anthroposemiosis itself) "there is no code"—even though, like sound waves on the side of nature, codes may play a supporting role and even result from the message.

In this perspective, criticism can contribute in its own right to bringing into explicit objectivity contributions of the understanding that have been left in a virtual state of exercise rather than expressly signified and recognized. This would be criticism at its best, criticism displaying the rich art of evaluating and analyzing with knowledge and propriety the works of civilization, especially art, music, and literature, wherein the free play of intellect and the full contrast of the objective to the biological and physical orders come into pre-eminence. Such a criticism, far from being equated with semiotics, would participate in the development of semiotics, a development drawing into its network of renvoi the whole of past thought, present science, and future civilization.

In this way the critical exercise will also contribute to, and perhaps even establish within semiotics, a formula more adequate to the full understanding of *anthropos* than any that has been devised heretofore.

6

PHYSIOSEMIOSIS AND
PHYTOSEMIOSIS

We noted in chapter 3 that Peirce, by bringing the action along with the being of signs into the focus of a thematic inquiry, took one of the decisive steps in establishing the full possibilities for developing a doctrine of signs. This step marks the difference between the contemporary development of semiotics and all earlier stages, historically speaking, of a move toward semiotic consciousness. For, while the being proper to signs exists actually only within the context of experience (in precisely the sense that experience presupposes cognition), the action that underlies this possible being by no means presupposes cognition.

How to understand the actions of signs outside the context of cognitive life? If this could be achieved, the scope of semiotics as a possible science would become as wide as could be, for it would be commensurate with an activity and type of causality coextensive with the physical universe. Such a "broader conception" of the sign, as Peirce called it, would embrace all four of the levels identified in this book, to wit, the two levels of cognitive semiosis (anthroposemiosis and zoösemiosis), and two lower levels of semiosis not dependent on cognition as such (phytosemiosis and physiosemiosis), as appears in the following passage (Peirce c.1907: 205–206):

> The action of a sign generally takes place between two parties, the *utterer* and the *interpreter*. They need not be persons; for a chameleon and many kinds of insects and even plants make their living by uttering signs, and

lying signs, at that. Who is the utterer of signs of the weather . . . ? However, every sign certainly conveys something of the general nature of thought, if not from a mind, yet from some repository of ideas, or significant forms, and if not to a person, yet to something capable of somehow 'catching on', . . . that is, of receiving not merely a physical, nor even merely a psychical dose of energy, but a significant meaning. In that modified, and as yet very misty, sense, then, we may continue to use the italicized words.

Peirce's remark (1905–1906: 5.448n) that "this universe is perfused with signs, if it is not composed exclusively of signs" may be regarded as a kind of capsule summary of this broader conception, and his much earlier enigmatic assertion (1868: 5.314) that "man is a sign" would be a kind of corollary.

But can this broader conception be justified? Is it warranted by the nature of semiosis? Clearly, the very attempt at such justification would require going beyond the bounds conventionally established for scientific thought, which we may say had already by Peirce's day more or less dogmatically embraced the view of nature as engaged exclusively in chance interactions of a brute force character.

Conventional boundaries as such, of course, had no interest for Peirce when the inquiry demanded their violation, and such seemed the case with the problem at hand. To Peirce, the fact that a sign always signifies something to or for another suggested the need to reconsider the taboo notion of final causality, or so-called teleology.[31]

At least in the context of the biological sciences, such a move was to some degree inevitable. Later biologists (for example, Simpson, Pittendrigh, and Tiffany 1957; Pittendrigh 1958; Mayr 1974, 1983) would prefer to speak of "teleonomy", to make the point that actual purpose in the individual sense is not necessary to account for the behavior (such as the rhythmic climbing of the female turtle onto the sand and laying its eggs) that the observer must ascribe to plan in nature in order to make scientific sense of the observations (a point also made by von Uexküll).

---

31. Ransdell (1977: 163) points out that Peirce expressly "thought of semiotic as precisely the development of a concept of final cause process and as a study of such processes", a fact that his would-be commentators so far have treated as "an embarrassment, a sort of intellectual club foot that one shouldn't be caught looking at, much less blatantly pointing out to others"–which explains "why the topic of final causation is so strangely absent in criticisms and explanations of Peirce's conception of semiotic and semiosis" despite its centrality in Peirce's own reflections and explanations.

For Poinsot, too, the question of final causality arises in the context of semiotic (1632a: Book I, Question 4, and editorial notes 10–12 thereon, pp. 174–178) but as expressly distinguished from the causality specific to the sign (see esp. 174/18–178/7), which is restricted neither to the order of actual existence nor to the order of intention (to signs as bearing an intention) and is operative even in chance events that signify as well virtually independently of any processes involving intention or cognition.

But, in the larger physical universe of atoms, stars, and intergalactic dust, even such a moderate version of teleology is extremely difficult to sustain as pertaining to the particles and interactions themselves, especially those of a more random sort such as meteor showers, the bombardment of cosmic rays, the dispersion of light, etc. True, there is the fact of stellar evolution and planetary formation, in relation to which the formation of the elements out of more primitive atomic materials and the distribution of matter seems to be law-governed in statistically determinable ways rather than random. This non-randomness led thinkers such as Henderson (1913: 305) to argue with considerable persuasiveness and empirical support that "physical science . . . no less than biological science appears to manifest teleology". But the "teleology" here, if such it can be called, appears to be entirely external to the interactions themselves.

The problem is that, before the advent of living matter and continuing in the inorganic environmental factors taken in their own right, the inorganic components themselves (no matter how much they may be modified and dominated by vital processes and organic symbioses in a gaia situation, the situation of a living planet), seem overwhelmingly to enter the process of cosmic evolution only indirectly, through the direct process of random or chance interactions. Once these have occurred, the inorganic components are inevitably redirected by the nature of the particles or bodies interacting and result, through this redirection, in processes of complexification and cosmic development overall. The consequent development overall, however, does not disguise the fact of the random foundation. This undeniable substructure of chance encounters in a realm of brute secondness seems to pose a barrier to any possible extension of semiosis beyond the boundaries of the living world.

Nonetheless, by linking the action of signs to future-oriented changes in the world of nature, Peirce had clearly pointed the way to what Sebeok called attention to in the early 1960s as "a vision of new and startling dimensions: the convergence of the science of genetics with the science of linguistics . . . in the larger field of communication studies". In this view (Sebeok 1968: 69):

> the genetic code must be regarded as the most fundamental of all semiotic networks and therefore as the prototype for all other signaling systems used by animals, including man. From this point of view, molecules that are quantum systems, acting as stable physical information carriers, zoösemiotic systems, and, finally, cultural systems, comprehending language, constitute a natural sequel of stages of ever more complex energy levels in a single universal evolution. It is possible, therefore, to describe language as well as living systems from a unified cybernetic standpoint . . . A mutual appreciation of genetics, animal communication studies,

and linguistics may lead to a full understanding of the dynamics of semiosis, and this may, in the last analysis, turn out to be no less than the definition of life.

This indeed is a grand vision. It falls, however, considerably short of the broader conception Peirce had in mind in linking the sign to final causality.[32] At the same time, it is probably as far as a conception of semiosis can effectively be made to reach on the basis of linking the causality proper to signs with any defensible notion of final causality.[33] The linkage, quite apart from the question of its correctness, is insufficient to establish the range of the connection required for semiosis to pervade nature all the way to its cosmic foundations. Thus, while the "new and startling vision" of Sebeok considerably propelled contemporary semiotics beyond the boundaries of a glottocentrically conceived anthroposemiosis and in the direction of considering sign processes as at work throughout the biological world, it still provided no ground for a notion of physiosemiosis, for seeing the action proper to signs as already at work in physical nature itself beyond the bounds of organic matter or prior to its advent.

To provide this further ground and to establish the Peircean broader conception of semiotics, therefore, would be the same thing. This other decisive step, taken together with the Peircean one of bringing the action along with the being of signs into thematic focus, is what is required to establish the full possibilities for a doctrine of signs.

This step depends on the further discovery that there is a more general causality at work in the sign than the final causality typical of the vital powers. This more general causality specifies vital activity but specifies also the causality at work in chance interactions of brute secondness. It is this causality, not final causality, that is the causality proper to the sign in its distinctive function of making present what it itself is not, for it is this causality, not final causality, that transforms, for example, accidental scratches into a clue leading the detective to the apprehension of the murderer.

---

32. While retaining my earlier reservations about Sebeok's stand from the strict perspective in which they were conceived (the origins of fully actual semiosis in cognition), I again find it necessary not merely to repeat but to expand upon and deepen the broad-gauge adjustments to that restricted perspective I had already introduced (Deely 1982a) in first considering systematically the notion of phytosemiotics introduced by Krampen in 1981.

In my first round of criticism (1978a), I considered Sebeok's then-singularly large view of semiotics too grand.

In my second round of criticism (1982a), I called it perhaps not grand enough.

Now I would like to strike out the "perhaps" and let it go at that, for the reasons developed in this chapter.

33. The qualification is a crucial one, for only a very limited range of the notions associated historically with the notion of "final causality" retain any claim to critical consideration today. See the discussion of this point in the editorial notes to Book I, Question 4 of the *Tractatus de Signis* (Poinsot 1632a).

The causality distinctive of semiosis, in its contrast with physical modes of causality, need not be goal-oriented in any intrinsic sense. On the contrary, it needs to be a causality equally able to ground sign-behavior in chance occurrences and planned happenings. On any construction, final causality cannot do this.

The decisive step in this regard was taken fully neither by Poinsot nor by Peirce. It can be taken from what is set forth in Poinsot's *Treatise on Signs* (1632a: Book I, Question 4, and Appendix C)[34] but only once the problematic of the sign as a whole has been redefined so as to make the action of signs equiprimordial with their being. Thus, taking the decisive step requires first that we straddle the work of both thinkers, even though the step to be taken is more immanent to what Peirce had in mind for semiotic than it is to anything Poinsot explicitly envisioned for the doctrine of signs. Here, where each of them in steps taken separately had come up short, in a doctrinal convergence between them, lies the basis for the decisive final step of extending semiotic understanding beyond the sphere of cognitive phenomena to the whole of nature itself. With this step, the broader conception Peirce dreamed of becomes realized.

To see how the dream becomes real, let us begin at the point where Peirce was tempted to despair of his broader conception. Then, by expanding outward from this point, removing step by step each of the reasons for a temptation to settle for a more restricted notion of the sign, we will be able to end up with a warranted version of the broader conception and of all four of the levels it implies.

Before there are actually signs, there are signs virtually, that is, there are beings and events so determined by other beings and events that, in their own activity as so determined, they determine yet further series of beings and events in such a way that the last terms in the series represent the first terms by the mediation of the middle terms. As Craik put it (1967:

---

34. As Powell wrote to me (letter of 16 December 1988): "the extension of extrinsic formal causality from specifier of vital powers, active and passive (Poinsot 1632a: Book I, Question 4), to *specifier of categorial relations* (Appendix C: 382/14ff.) *concerns precisely physiosemiosis.* For the specification of categorial relations extends to the universe at large . . .".

Concerning this Appendix C, we had already explained in 1985 (p. 450) that we had added it to the Books of Poinsot's *Treatise* with a view to the questions of research strategies, "but in a very specific way. It is provided to ground in Poinsot's text the Peircean idea of extending semiotic understanding beyond the sphere of cognitive phenomena to the whole of nature itself as a network virtually semiosic in character . . . . The discussion in this Third Appendix . . . extends and completes the discussion of objective causality in Book I, Question 4, of the *Treatise on Signs.*"

Moreover, in Peirce's work a tendency toward what is set forth in Book I, Question 4, specifically as completed by the ideas of the editorially added Appendix C, is definitely marked, inasmuch as Peirce groped in the direction of a distinction between "ideal" and "final" causality, along the lines Poinsot had earlier established for semiotics under the rubric of "objective" or "extrinsic formal" causality. See the remarks in the next chapter, where Peirce is considered in the context of the history of semiotics.

59), "It is only the sensitive 'receptors' on matter, and means of intercommunication . . . which are lacking".

The actions and relations in such a series are actually at the level of secondness. But, even at that level, they anticipate the intervention of cognition and experience: they so stand to one another in relations of determining and being determined that they constitute a *pattern of knowability*, a *virtual* thirdness, which, should it come to be actually known in some context of experience, will exhibit precisely that element of thirdness, that irreducible elemental type of representation, constitutive of the sign relation.

The years 1908 and 1909, in this respect, seem to have been a period of crisis and some despondency for Peirce in his project of establishing semiotic. In 1908, in a letter to Lady Welby, he tossed in despair his famous "sop to Cerberus", introducing the notion of "person" into his definition of sign (1908a: 88–89):

> I define a sign as anything which is so determined by something else, called its object, and so determines an effect upon a person, which effect I call its interpretant, that the latter is thereby mediated by the former. My insertion of the term 'upon a person' is a sop to Cerberus, because I despair of making my own broader conception understood.

If, as is to be expected, the term "person" here is equivalent to "human being", then the term "sign" so qualified would be restricted to the region of anthroposemiosis. In order to reach Peirce's "broader conception", therefore, it is necessary to remove this qualification and consequent restriction, which we may do with the following abstract formula: a sign will be any A so *determined by* a B that in *determining* C that C is mediately determined by B. Thus, B determines A, and, precisely in the respect in which

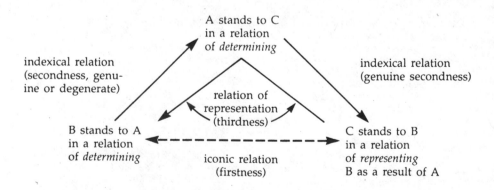

FIGURE 4. *Abstract Version of the Semiotic Triangle*

B has determined it, A determines C. Therefore C, in being immediately determined by A, is at the same time mediately determined by B. We see here the most primitive and abstract form of the semiotic triangle that is behind the "pyramid of anthroposemiosis" looked at in the last chapter.

In other words, C is passive to A in just the way that A is passive to B; but, precisely by reason of being passive in this way, C is virtually active respecting both A and B as a representation or representative element. Let B be rain and A the clouds whence the rain precipitates, and C be the experience of an organism caught in the rain. The effect of being caught in the rain will establish for the organism a new relation to B whereby A will henceforward exist for C as a sign of B, thus:

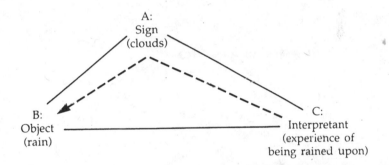

FIGURE 5. *Concretization of the Triangle within Animal Experience*

Or let A be the bone of a dinosaur buried in what we saw in chapter 4 would become a garden, and let B be the dinosaur long dead. C in this case would not be the effect of the bone on the gardener, for that, as we saw in concluding Chapter 4, did not result in any actualization of the transcendental relation—the representative element—of the bone to the dinosaur. The effect of the bone on the gardener did not make of this relation a sign. Nonetheless, the element representative in this respect was there, identical with the bone, but needing to be actualized. It was there, of a piece with the bone in physical being, but virtually distinct therefrom. When the paleontologist came along, however, this virtuality was actualized. The perceptual effect of the bone on the paleontologist, but not on the gardener, triggered the virtual element whereby the bone actually represents the dinosaur. Hence Poinsot's formula (1632a: 126/3–5): "It suffices to be a sign virtually in order to signify in act".

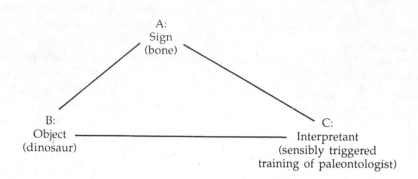

FIGURE 6.   *Concretization of the Triangle within Human Experience*

Thus, again, let B be the dinosaur, A the bone, and C a geological formation in which the bone has been turned to stone.

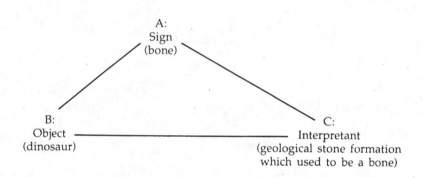

FIGURE 7.   *Concretization of the Triangle within the Environment*

In this case the interpretant is a physical rather than a psychical structure but one that has been so determined by A as to represent through A also B. In this way the interaction is a virtual semiosis, that is, a series of interactions at the level of secondness that, at the same time, provides an actual pathway through time whereby it is possible that what happened long ago might be partially understood. The present, indeed, from such a standpoint, might be regarded as a mosaic of traces from the past, each providing the starting point, for a sufficiently knowledgeable present observer, of a journey into what used to be. Notice that it is not necessary that such possibility be actualized in order for it to be possible. Nor is it merely "possible" in some abstract, conceptual sense. Our example, for example, exists in the geological formation virtually. The bone (A), or the rock formation that used to be a bone (C), is "not a sign formally but virtually and fundamentally", as Poinsot puts it (1632a: 12–18):

> For since the rationale of moving or stimulating the mind remains, which comes about through the sign insofar as it is something representative even if the relation of substitution for the signified does not remain, the sign is able to exercise the functions of substituting without the relation.

We see, thus, at once: how the interpretant is fundamental to the semiosis, that the interpretant need not be a psychological state or idea, and why the interpretant is itself a sign or link in what Eco calls the chain of "unlimited semiosis".

Since it is through its fundament that the sign is a representation, and it is through this being of representation that the sign is involved in the brute force interactions of secondness and physical existence, it follows that the virtuality of signs is present and operative throughout the realm of nature, and not just among the animals where signs exist and function in their proper being actually as well as virtually.[35]

Moreover, this virtual semiosis prior to any cognitive life is not restricted to passive reflections in present being of past interactions, such as we have considered so far. Virtual semiosis is also at work in the ways that present interactions anticipate future conditions radically different from what presently obtains. In other words, present effects are virtual signs not just retrospectively, but prospectively as well. They portend, and do so in two ways. First of all, in any given interaction of bodies, over and above the resultant relations of cause and effect (acting and being acted upon), there is the fact that each of the bodies involved interprets and twists the action according to its own intrinsic nature. In this way, as Powell puts it (1986: 300), "the extrinsic specification of causal relations always reveals indirectly the intrinsic species of the bodies which are their extrinsic specifying causes". For example, if I strike the armor of a tank, a porcelain bowl, or the trunk of a tree with a hammer, the relation of agent to patient is in all three cases the same; or, as Powell again puts it (ibid.), "spatio-temporal/real causal relational systems do not have determinate intrinsic species as bodies do". However, owing to the intrinsically diverse properties of steel, porcelain, and wood pulp, the effect will be likewise diversified in each case.

---

35. Peirce 1908b: 8.343: "it is necessary to distinguish the *Immediate Object*, or the Object as the Sign represents it, from the *Dynamical Object*, or really efficient but not immediately present Object. It is likewise requisite to distinguish the *Immediate Interpretant*, i.e., the Interpretant represented or signified in the Sign, from the *Dynamic Interpretant*, or effect actually produced on the mind by the Sign; and both of these from the *Normal Interpretant*, or effect that would be produced on the mind by the Sign after sufficient development of thought. . . . I do not say that these divisions are enough." Cf. 1909: 8.314; 1904.

Thus, dyadic interactions, as extrinsically specified by the bodies involved at the level of secondness, also project a virtual level of thirdness that anticipates changes in future states respecting the interactions occurring here and now. And the measure of these interactions occurs through precisely the same type of causality operative in the sign, whereby it achieves indifference to the being and non-being, presently considered, of what is signified.[36]

Here, however, in the direction of future states, the virtuality of the semiosis is more complicated. The reason is that the direct deflection of the results of the interactions itself can lead to changes in the immediate constitution of what does the interacting—as, for example, when one of the interactants is destroyed by the interaction, or when the interaction triggers a new phase in the development of one of the interactants, or when a specifically new type of being (such as a new atomic elementary formation) results from the interaction. Here, Peirce's idea of scientific laws existing as habits in nature as a whole would seem to find, as it were, a semiotic grounding. For, over and above the individual interactions of bodies, there is a macroformation of the universe that takes place directionally, as it were, toward the establishment of conditions under which virtual semioses move always closer to actuality.

Out of cosmic dust, stellar systems form through subatomic, atomic, and molecular interactions. At various stages of the process, new elements not previously given precipitate from the interactions, even as now on

---

36. Poinsot (1632a: 382/4–26) extends extrinsic formal causality, that is, the objective causality of semiosis, from specification of vital powers to categorial or physical relations as such, in the following manner: "distinction has to be made between the terminus understood most formally in the rationale of an opposed terminus, and the terminus understood fundamentally on the side of the subjective being founding this rationale of terminating. In the former way a terminus concurs in a specification purely terminatively, but not by causing that specification, because so considered it is a pure terminus and simultaneous by nature and in cognition with the relation; therefore as such it is not a specifying cause, because a cause is not naturally simultaneous with but prior to its effect. If it is considered in the latter way, the terminus stands as an extrinsic formal cause and specifies in the manner of an object, and in this way a single specifying rationale of the relation arises from the foundation and terminus together, inasmuch as the foundation contains the terminus within itself by a proportion and power; for it is not relative to a given terminus unless it is a specific fundament, and conversely. In this way, to the extent that they are mutually proportioned, terminus and foundation together bring about a single rationale specifying a relation which postulates both a specific foundation and a specific terminus corresponding thereto.

"From these remarks one can further gather what a formal terminus is in the rationale of something specifying. For although specifically different relations can be anchored to the materially same terminus, yet they cannot be anchored to the *formally* same terminus. But the formal specifying rationale in a terminus is understood in accordance with a correspondence and adequate proportion to its fundament. . . . Wherefore, as regards the specifying of any relation, in just the way that the fundament is understood under the final rationale of the grounding of the relation, so the terminus of the relation is understood under the proportion and correspondence of the terminating."

See further in Index 4 to the *Treatise* (the Index Rerum/Index of Terms and Propositions) the entries under "Object", pp. 552–554, beginning with no. 4, referring the whole text to extrinsic formal causality. Also see the entries for "Foundation", p. 539.

earth we can in laboratories bring into being a few elements not yet existent in nature itself. These elements, in turn, prove essential to the formation in planetary systems of the conditions under which living beings become possible, and these beings, in turn, further modify the planetary conditions so that successive generations of living beings are incompatible with the original conditions of life. Oxygen, essential for life on this planet now, for example, was originally introduced as a waste product of living beings who neither needed nor could survive within a heavily oxygenated atmosphere.

Through this entire series of intersecting and often conflicting processes resulting in cosmic evolution over-all, the specificity and identity of any given process at each step is guaranteed not by individual bodies but by systems of commonly specified real relations between bodies, that is, by specifically identifiable categorially determined systems of ontological relations. Within these systems individual bodies *further* determine their immediate interactions according to their own intrinsic natures. In the case of organisms this determination in turn depends on a whole sub-system of interactions indisputably semiotic in nature, as Sebeok has pointed out (1977a, 1988, 1989a). The relational systems as a whole and the interactions within them form throughout a single web of at least virtual semiosis, governed at each point by the objective causality of the sign virtually at work throughout. This causality corresponds to the plan in von Uexküll's distinction (1934: 42–46) between goal and plan in nature and is, as Powell points out (1988a: 180, 186), "prior to the well-known Aristotelian four causes, the agent, the final, the formal, and the material cause":

> It is precisely the function of extrinsic formal causality to displace the agent and final causes by a more elementary cause which is not committed to explaining how interaction could be understood. Thus the solar system is explained as a mechanism specified by extrinsic formal causes without needing any explanation by agent causes (let alone by final causes which have not been recognized by science since the seventeenth century). For Einstein's general theory of relativity precisely eliminated gravitational forces from explanation of the solar system, by substituting the curvature of space time for gravitational forces (Hawking 1988: 29–30). Now gravitational forces are agent causes, whereas the curved space-time that governs the path of the earth around the sun is an excellent example of extrinsic formal causality . . . because that path consists of specified temporal relations between the earth and the other bodies of the solar system . . . plain cases of extrinsic formal causality.

Thus, Peirce's discouragement at establishing his broadest conception of semiosis proves unnecessary,[37] once it is understood that the specification

---

37. Likewise unnecessary was his desperate earlier resort to panpsychism as a ploy for introducing thirdness into the realm of inorganic matter (1892: 6.158, 1892a: 6.268), which yet failed to solve the problem of *experienced* thirdness (c.1909: 6.322) as required by the sign for its proper and formal being.

of categorial relations in the universe at large already puts into play the causality upon which the action of signs depends: already at the level of their fundaments, signs are virtually present and operative in the dyadic interactions of brute force, weaving together in a single fabric of virtual relations the future and the past of such interactions.

This is semiosis, but semiosis of a specific kind. I propose that we call it *physiosemiosis*, so as to bring out by the very name the fact that it is a question here of a process as broad as the physical universe itself. For this process is at work in all parts of it as the foundation of those higher, more distinctive levels of the same process that come into existence as the conditions of physical being themselves make possible the successively higher levels first of life, and then of cognitive life. Thus, the definition of semiosis is not just coextensive with the definition of life but broader than it.

Nonetheless, the transformation of physiosemiosis within specifically living interactions, even prior to any question of cognition as such, is dramatic, and requires a specifically identifying label. For physiosemiosis simply links the intelligibility of past and future, while looking to the future beyond interacting individuals only accidentally,[38] whereas the semiosis virtual to living matter is essentially oriented at once to the preservation as well as the propagation of the units interacting, and is thereby essentially future-oriented.[39]

It is probable that orientation to the future is operative in semiosis from the first. Certainly this is true if Henderson's unorthodox early view (1913: 305) that "physical science . . . no less than biological science appears to manifest teleology" ultimately proves correct.[40] Nonetheless, the above distinction between physiosemiosis, which depends on chance

---

38. I say that physiosemiosis looks to the future only in a comparatively accidental or tangential way, inasmuch as, in the case of inorganic agents, which cause only as they are moved, "from the very movement that they undergo they are ordered to producing effects. And similarly in all cases where a good of any kind accrues to the cause from the effect" (Aquinas c.1265–1267: q. 7. art. 10), such as Powell's example (1986: 297) of the senselessness of saying that "the causal relation whereby one cat scratches out the eye of the other is specified by a final cause". For even though "one and the same motion is a 'good blow' for the one scratching out and a 'disaster' for the one losing its eye", the good (and the "disaster") pertains directly to the individual circumstances of the cats, not to their specific natures as belonging to a determinate biological population.
39. Furthermore, in the case of anthroposemiosis, the preservation and generation of culture is future-oriented *beyond* mere biological propagation, a point that completes the grand view of a progression through past-future relations from physiosemiosis to anthroposemiosis. This is a progression, however, in which the successive levels of transcendence do not fully leave behind, but rather contain and continue according to varying requirements, the previous levels.
40. If the power of Henderson's arguments was outweighed by their unorthodoxy in the scientific community of his day, that is rapidly ceasing to be the case in the age of Gaia (Lovelock 1979), where the recognition at last of delicate interdependencies within our own planetary ecology and between that ecology and the solar and cosmic radiation through which our planet moves have begun at long last to become themselves objectified as well as physical.

events for achieving its future orientation, and the semiosis of living matter, which essentially turns chance events toward the future, suggests the
boundary line between physiosemiosis and phytosemiosis, the "semiotics
of plant life", as Krampen calls it, or of living matter in general.

Krampen, basing his view on the work of J. von Uexküll, uses a con-
trastive "method of opposition" to show how the meaning-factors work in
an environment which lacks the Umwelt-structure introduced by cognitive
interactions (cf. T. von Uexküll 1982: 5–6). "Using the example of the leaves
of an oak tree", Krampen remarks (1981: 195), "Jakob von Uexküll shows
how phytosemiosis functions":

> One of the meaning factors, as far as oak leaves are concerned, is the
> rain. Falling raindrops follow precise physical laws governing the behav-
> ior of liquids upon striking a leaf. In this case, according to Jakob von
> Uexküll, the leaf is the 'receiver of m', coupled with the m factor 'rain'
> by a 'meaning rule'. The form of the leaves is such that it accommodates
> the physical laws governing the behavior of liquids. The leaves work to-
> gether by forming cascades in all directions in order to distribute the rain
> water on the ground for optimal use by the roots. To put it in more com-
> mon semiotic terminology, the leaf's form is the signifier and the physical
> behavior of the raindrop is the signified. The code coupling leaf and rain-
> drop is the oak tree's need of liquid for the transport of nourishing salts
> into its cells.

Of course, from the point of view of present planetary conditions,
plants have played and continue to play, especially in the great rain-
forests, a crucial evolutionary role, one that began with bringing about an
oxidizing atmosphere (about a billion years ago), then sustained ever after-
ward the basic matrix required for the development and continuance of all
higher forms of animal life. Perhaps by reason of his reliance on von
Uexküll,[41] perhaps for reasons of his own, Krampen considers this situation
only synchronically, in terms of its end-development, as follows (1981:
197):

> There is one fundamental rule of correspondence between humans and
> animals on the one hand and plants on the other, this being of critical
> importance for life: Plants produce the oxygen all humans and animals
> breathe. In other words, the life of plants corresponds as a counterpoint
> to the breathing lungs of humans and animals as a point.

---

41. By relying on Kantian notions of fixed formal a-prioris to explain the difference between
goal and plan in nature, J. von Uexküll deprived himself of a philosophical framework containing the dynamic notion of objective causality as specificative of physical interactions in
nature. This helps to account for the fact that, throughout his life, he remained anachronistic-
ally opposed to the idea of evolution, sometimes even justifying this historically idiosyncratic
conceptual opposition on the thin semantic grounds of etymology.

But, of course, there is considerably more to be considered here than a merely external correspondence and exploitive dependency. Here again we reach one of those points where the semiotic point of view exceeds the bounds of glottocentrism and in this sense manifests its affinity more with the ontological veins of ancient and medieval thought than with the nominalistic strains of renaissance and modern philosophy. Consider the following text, which is singularly uncharacteristic of the mainstream of modern philosophy as it waxes increasingly glottocentric in contemporary times. (I choose this text in part for its fortuitous extension of the phytosemiotic image of the oak tree cited above from Krampen on the basis of von Uexküll's work.) The text is from a turn-of-the-century philosopher, Jules Lachelier (1933: XVIII-XIX):

> It seems to me, when I am at Fontainebleau, that I sympathize in all my energies with the powerful vitality of the trees which surround me. I am too encrusted in my own form to be able to reproduce their form; yet, on well considering the matter, it does not seem unreasonable to hold that all forms of being sleep more or less deeply buried in the ground of each being. Under the sharp contours of my human form any careful observer could see the vaguer contours of 'animality', which veils in turn the even more fluid and incomplete form of simple organic life. Now one of the possible determinations of organic life is tree, which engenders in turn the oak tree. So the "being of an oak tree" is somewhere hidden in the foundations of my being, and may even strive sometimes to emerge and appear in its turn *dias in luminis oras* [in the upper world of light]—but humanity, which has gotten ahead of it, prevents it from doing so and blocks its way.[42]

This text strikes us in our cultural milieu as something idiosyncratic or even bizarre. Yet in truth it is no more than a faithful echo of the older traditions of the Western philosophical mainstream. We need only recall the reflections in this area common to Greek and Latin thought, before the unique development of modern philosophy effectively shifted concern away from natural being to the universe of human discourse in such ways as effectively to close the range of philosophy within the conventionalized realms of human culture.

---

42. "Il me semble, quand je suis à Fontainebleau, que je sympathise de toutes mes forces avec la vitalité puissante des arbres qui m'entourent. Quant à réproduire jusqu'à leur forme, je suis sans doute trop encroûté dans la mienne pour cela; mais, en y réfléchissant bien, il ne me paraît pas déraisonnable de supposer que toutes les formes de l'existence dorment plus ou moins profondément ensevelies au fond de chaque être; car sous les traits bien arrêtés de la forme humaine dont je suis revêti. Un oeil un peu perçant doit reconnaître sans peine le contour plus vague de l'*animalité*, qui voile à son tour la forme encore plus flottante et plus indécise de la simple *organisation*: or l'une des déterminations possibles de l'organisation est l'*arboréité*, qui engendre à son tour la *chênéité*. Donc la *chênéité* est cachée quelque part dans mon fond, et peut être quelquefois tentée d'en sortir et de paraître à son tour *dias in luminis oras*, bien que l'humanité, qui a pris les devants sur elle, le lui défende, et lui barre le chemin."

According to this older, broader mainstream, the life of the plant exists within the animal itself precisely as base and part of its proper life. That is to say, there is a common life principle that is the first principle of all planetary life as such. I quote from a typical medieval commentary (Aquinas, c.1266–1272) on Aristotle's original conception (c.330BC) of "psychology" as the science of living things:

> Aristotle defines the primary principle of life, which is called the vegetative psyche or soul; in plants this is the entire soul, while in animals it is only a part of the soul . . . . To understand his definition, it must be seen that there is a definite order among the three operations of the plant soul. For its first activity is taking food, through which the living thing preserves its existence. The second and more perfect activity is growth, by which the living thing develops both in size and vital energy. But the third, most perfect, and fulfilling activity is reproduction, through which something already as it were existing perfected in its own right, transmits to another being and perfection. For, as Aristotle observes in Book IV of his *Meteorology* (c. 1, 4–18), anything achieves its greatest perfection when it is able to make another such as it itself is. Since therefore things are appropriately defined and named by their outcome, whereas the fulfillment of the activity of plant life is the generation of another living being, it follows that it will be a proper definition of the first principle of life, that is to say, of the plant soul, if we define it as *what is generative of another like itself on the plan of being alive.*[43]

This ancient way of conceptualizing the nature and essence of life in general, and of plant life in particular, coincides fairly squarely, in contemporary terms, with our understanding of the genetic code. Such a conceptualization places a wholly unexpected back-drop of tradition behind Dr. Sebeok's bold claim that, if indeed the genetic code is a semiotic system (such that genetics and linguistics, as codes, subtend the upper and lower reaches of semiosis), then indeed in the full perspective of Western philosophical tradition "a full understanding of the dynamics of semiosis" would, in the last analysis, "turn out to be no less than the definition of life".

---

43. Liber II, lect. 9, n. 347: "Definit ipsam primam animam, quae dicitur anima vegetabilis; quae quidem in plantis est anima, in animalibus pars animae. . . . Ad cuius definitionis intellectum, sciendum est, quod inter tres operationes animae vegetabilis, est quidam ordo. Nam prima eius operatio est nutritio, per quam salvatur aliquid ut est. Secunda autem perfectior est augmentum, quo aliquid proficit in maiorem perfectionem, et secundum quantitatem et secundum virtutem. Tertia autem perfectissima et finalis est generatio per quam aliquid iam quasi in seipso perfectum existens, alteri esse et perfectionem tradit. Tunc enim unumquodque maxime perfectum est, ut in *quarto Meteororum* dicitur (8), cum potest facere alterum tale, quale ipsum est. Quia igitur iustum est, ut omnia definiantur et denominentur a fine, finis autem operum animae vegetabilis est generare alterum tale quale ipsum est, sequitur quod ipsa sit conveniens definitio primae animae, scilicet vegetabilis, *ut sit generativa alterius similis secundum speciem.*"

At the same time, as our above remarks have suggested, the full understanding of the dynamics of semiosis also turn out to include yet more extension than the definition of life. For phytosemiosis in turn needs to be seen as an extension and specification at a new level of the more general process and processes of physiosemiosis, upon which plants too depend.

In this perspective it becomes also clear that the proposal of Krampen (1981: 187)

> to establish phytosemiotics, i.e., the semiotics of plants, as an area of inquiry into sign processes, parallel and on an equal footing with anthroposemiotics, the study of human communication, and zoösemiotics, the study of sign processes occurring within and between species of animals, the three areas forming together the discipline of biosemiotics

is a reasonable ramification of the "vision of new and startling dimensions" to which Sebeok pointed in the early 1960s.

From the point of view of the analogy between linguistics and genetics, and within the dialectic of concepts set up thereby, the establishment of phytosemiotics alongside anthroposemiotics and zoösemiotics completes a tryptic. Within this analogy, phytosemiotics has already a right to existence, its place marked out in advance. What is surprising, perhaps, is less Krampen's proposal than the fact that twenty years elapsed between Sebeok's statement on the dimensions of semiotics and the concrete advancement of such a proposal. Far from being the aberrant proposal it seemed when viewed from a standpoint of more or less explicit glottocentrism, it appears in an integrally semiotic perspective as an important and daring step in the dialectical maturation of the doctrine of signs.

This is not to say that the notion is without difficulties or that its final status vis-à-vis anthroposemiosis and zoösemiosis is assured. In fact, even in Krampen's original proposal, two quite distinct possibilities for the definition of phytosemiotics are outlined. The first and explicit scheme is for a relatively autonomous area of inquiry, "on an equal footing with anthroposemiotics and zoösemiotics", as Krampen puts it, using opposition as "the method by which the specificity of plant semiosis can be shown" (p. 192). By the use of this method, Krampen is able to show, as the ancient philosophers also argued, that (p. 203) "many life processes within the animal and human organisms function according to the principle of the vegetative world, i.e., according to the principle of phytosemiotics", although of course "the phytosemiotic level is contained within the zoösemiotic one at a new level of complexity" (T. von Uexküll 1982: 5–6).

Rich as are the results of this method in Krampen's hands, I am not convinced that they succeed in establishing phytosemiotics on an equal footing. Or, to put it another way, I am not convinced that the communication among plants and between plants and the physical environment and the communication between plants and animals is, on the side of the plants themselves, fully an actual process of semiosis, such as it certainly is on the side of the animals.

My hesitations here are an extension of the distinction, as we have drawn it above, between virtual and actual semiosis. This extension can be couched in the form of a distinction between communication, which is virtually semiotic, and actual signification proper. The two have in common the nature of being thoroughly relational states of affairs—in addition to which all conscious communication, whether self-reflective or not, within or between organisms, is by means of signification. But, although it is true that all relational phenomena are communicative, it is not conversely true that all communicative events adequately realize, even when they virtually contain, the triadic character required for an action fully semiosic. All relation involves signification potentially, but this becomes actual only through the intervention of cognition.

With these distinctions in mind, the situation of semiosis in the context of communication phenomena (relations) can be outlined thus:

SEMIOSIC ACTIVITY

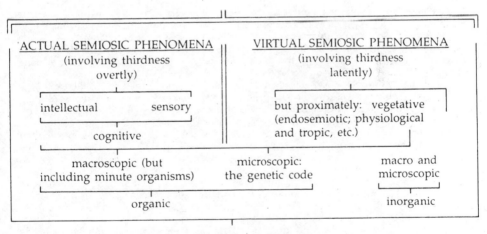

FIGURE 8. *Semiosic Activity and Relational Phenomena*

In this scheme, the dynamics of semiosis in the strict and full, or overt, sense are co-extensive with the dynamics of cognitive life rather than with the dynamics of life itself. My original objection (1978a) to Sebeok's proposal that the genetic code is already a semiotic network was based on this consideration.[44]

At the same time, the genetic code is unquestionably a communication network and a communication network whereby the present shapes the future, both in its being and in its virtual knowability. Through the genetic code the limitless possibilities of organic life are opened up, just as through the linguistic code the infinity of cognitive life is rendered possible in anthroposemiosis—which is, after all, "le coeur de l'analogie", as Sebeok pointed out.[45]

Although there are hierarchical distinctions to be made in the levels of semiosis as well as circular feed-back laces between the levels, the picture that now emerges shows the problem to be mainly one of according proper emphases. First of all, the quasi-presemiosic (the "merely virtually semiotic") character of plant life, or still more of the processes of formation of star and planetary systems in the first place, needs to be given due weight. Second, what needs to be given due weight is the remarkable ordering whereby semiosis (thanks to the inorganic processes of planetary formation and the organic processes of vegetable life), which is virtually present and operative throughout, first becomes sustained actually in its proper possibilities, then grows both in size and vitality, and finally transforms into itself (at least by tendency and right of domination) all that pre-

---

44. The theoretical attempt that I made (1978a, 1982a) to restrict semiosis to the cognitive order brought everything under the rubric of semiotics inasmuch as all things are in principle knowable: anything can become an object of awareness, and any object of awareness can come to function as a sign. The basis for attempting theoretically to restrict semiosis to the order of actual cognition, thus, was the consideration that only cognition renders anything actually signifying this way or that way here and now.

But any attempt to restrict semiosis to cognition falls short at the level of theory for the reason that nature and culture mutually penetrate one another in the constitution of experience, so that the objects of experience *also* reveal themselves more suited to some significations than to others in any given context of inquiry. The objective sphere reveals itself as neither closed nor closable upon itself absolutely. The subjectivity both of the knower and of things known (with all their respective virtualities that exceed the actual semiosis of any given moment or case and moreover surround and exert an influence upon even the actual semiosis here and now) seeps into and permeates the objectivity of experience. The full semiosis of experience, thus, is never merely actual, but is suffused at every moment with elements and factors passing in and out of varying degrees of actuality and consciousness through the virtualities that remain in their own right semiosic (whether rooted primarily in the psychic or the physical side of subjectivity).

45. Sebeok 1974a: 108–109: "le fond du problème de l'analogie entre code génétique et code linguistique est en réalité très différent quand on le prend d'un point de vue linguistique. Le langage est un mécanisme très particulier, organisé de manière hiérarchique. Cette organisation hiérarchique est généralement désignée sous le nom de dualité, mais en réalité ce terme prête à confusion car il signifie essentiellement que l'on a un ensemble de sous-systèmes, et que le sous-système de base comporte un répertoire universel de traits binaires. C'est ce que les linguistes appellent des traits distinctifs (distinctive features), traits qui sont en eux-mêmes dépourvus de signification, mais à l'aide desquels on peut fabriquer un nombre infini de phrases, lesquelles forment un autre sous-système. Pour ce qui est de l'ensemble des systèmes de communication des organismes, ceci constitue un phénomène

ceded and once lay outside its actualized sphere. As Henderson remarked (1913: 312):

> The properties of matter and the course of cosmic evolution are now seen to be intimately related to the structure of the living being and its activities; they become, therefore, far more important in biology than has been previously suspected. For the whole evolutionary process, both cosmic and organic, is one, and the biologist may now rightly regard the universe in its very essence as biocentric.

Some recent speculations in physics (for example, Wheeler 1984) seem to bear out this point.

In any event, if it is true that "things are appropriately defined and named by their outcome", the semiotist is entitled to regard the universe in its very essence as 'semiocentric'. The "new and startling vision" of the sixties, which at first seemed too grand, proves, after all, not grand enough.

The post-modern era that semiotics introduces is no longer ontocentric as were classical and Latin times, neither anthropocentric as the renaissance nor glottocentric as the moderns, but semiocentric. Hence we can complete and complement the once-famous maxim of Aristotle, "anima est quoddammodo omnia" ("the soul in a certain way is all things"), by adding: "in a certain way, all things are semiotic" ("omnia sunt quodammodo semiotica"). That is, in a certain way (*quodammodo*), because of semiosis at work throughout the whole of nature transcendentally and virtually, inasmuch as physical nature sustains itself through interactions which also determine the possibilities of what is there to be known on the environmental side or in the physical dimension of objects within experience, as well as ontologically and integrally within experience itself as sustaining the network of objects as such (the Umwelt) in the first place.

Not only can anything signify through cognition, and not only through cognition can anything fully signify, but, also phenomena not in themselves actually semiotic are nonetheless entangled in semiosic virtualities. Such is the situation that has to be accounted for. We have to take account not only of the fact that all things become semiotic once an awareness of them, however partial, is acquired, but also of the fact that

---

unique, car nulle part ailleurs dans le monde animal on ne trouve trace d'une telle organisation hiérarchique. Le code génétique, si je le comprends bien, fonctionne de manière analogue. On a quatre unités de base qui sont en elles-mêmes dépourvues de signification, mais qui se combinent en des unités plus grandes, lesquelles se combinent en unités encore plus grandes qui, finalement, donnent lieu à un nombre infini de suites. C'est là le coeur de l'analogie, mais Jakobson est allé encore plus loin et a trouvé des analogies beaucoup plus fines, et je suis un peu gêné de devoir ajouter qu'il se réfère là explicitement à Monod."

all things in the process of becoming objectified work as if to have a say in the semioticity of their objectification. They not only respond to the web they are caught in, they also make the web respond to what it has caught.

Semiosis is above all an *assimilative* interactive process, especially as manifested in a form of life, but not only there. Semiosis is the process whereby phenomena originating anywhere in the universe signify virtually in their present being also their past and their future and begin the further process of realizing these virtualities especially when life intervenes and, within life, when cognition supervenes. The process does not begin with the cognition, it merely enters a further phase, a new magnitude of thirdness.

Let me comment, finally, on the second of the two possibilities for the definition of phytosemiotics I see outlined in Krampen's work, namely, the study of plants from the point of view of their symbiosis with animals. From this point of view, phytosemiotics would be defined as the study of the peculiar dependencies of animal upon plant life and of the benefits to human life in particular that could be derived from such a study. The method of opposition used by Krampen would necessarily form a substantial part and lay the foundations for this study. "This semiotic analysis", Krampen remarks (1981: 192), "may well form the positive scientific basis lacking so far in the conservationist activities that have, until now, largely been based on negation and ideology." And yet, viewed in this way, phytosemiotics would be, to borrow an older terminology, a study subalternate to rather than on an equal footing with zoösemiotics and anthroposemiotics.

Since this definition is in my opinion unquestionably valid in establishing phytosemiotics as an important and new semiotic perspective or field of inquiry and since, furthermore, it includes the methods and results of the alternative definition, I might summarize by saying that from Krampen's work I am convinced of phytosemiotics, but not of its equal footing with zoösemiotics or still less with anthroposemiotics. There seems to me a basic sense in which semiosis is hierarchical, a series of irreducible levels or zones that are integrally actualized only in the final layer that folds back, as it were, and assimilates the previous levels into itself so as to give them their final being as semiosic.[46] In either event, from the point of view

---

46. An analogous idea is expressed in what T. von Uexküll (1982: 7) calls "the specific anthroposemiotic process of envelopment. Only man can add to what he sees, hears, feels, and smells something that he knows. With this knowledge, I do not mean just memories of former experience which one can find also with animals and even with plants—but, as Piaget shows impressively, socially-established and socially-controlled ideas about an objective world, its natural objects and proceedings. This objective world is a construct of our imagination. We cannot see it, nor hear it, nor feel or taste it. It belongs to a realm which passes all sensoric conception. But we project it into our sensoric conceptions, and into that which we see, hear, feel, or taste.

of an anthroposemiosis that has become transparent to itself and grounded in principle, it remains that "the vegetative world is nevertheless structured according to a base semiotics which cuts across all living beings, plants, animals, and humans alike" (Krampen 1981: 203).

With the notion of phytosemiotics, then, Krampen has outlined a new area important even to the future of semiotic development (Krampen 1981: 208):

> Despite the impression of progress raised by the constant introduction of new and sophisticated tools between human effectors or receptors and the human Umwelt, the human organism cannot escape the basic vegetative rules of endosemiotics and remains locked together with plants by a mutual rule of correspondence: If men cease to care for plants, i.e., cease to understand their meaning factors and the meaning rules at the basis of their formation rules, they will asphyxiate themselves. As Thure von Uexküll has put it: 'Man is led, from his extravagant position as the observer positioned outside nature and as its unscrupulous exploiter, back into nature, in which he must arrange himself for better or worse.' Phytosemiotics can help to improve this arrangement.

At the same time, phytosemiotics marks not the final step but only a penultimate one in reaching the outlines of the full extent possible for the doctrine of signs.

We have now seen that the Peircean idea of extending semiotic understanding beyond the sphere of cognitive phenomena to the whole of nature itself, as a network virtually semiosic in character, had already been grounded in Poinsot's original treatise on semiotic foundations. We have likewise seen that the development of the doctrine of signs, drawing on

---

"We have learned and practiced this complicated intellectual construction of an objective world with objects and proceedings as the signified contents of our anthroposemiotic signs since childhood within the social environment in which we grow up. It is therefore not astonishing that we share this result—just this objective world—with all people who have learned and practiced the same intellectual process of construction for anthroposemiotic sign processes. This does not mean, however, that we share our objective world with all men, and even less that we share it with all living beings". We have seen this in chapter 5.

"The objective worlds in which Indian clans in the tropical forests of the Amazon or Australian aborigines live differ considerably from the objective world of Americans or Europeans of the industrial age."

The point is (p. 13) that "the human world is an observer's world. But we must choose and we can choose between a world of naive or of participant observation; this choice will determine our understanding of animals, plants, and human beings".

This choice will also determine our understanding finally of the physical universe conceived environmentally in general. For it is always perforce from within experience that the totality of the universe forms in our conception, including our notion of "thing": it is not a question of a naive or misleading belief "that neutral objects exist independently of signs and sign systems", but of what the signs indicate about the objects they systematically reveal, to wit, whether or not they exist in subjective as well as objective ways, or objectively only, and so forth.

contemporary experience and standing as well on the shoulders of the giants who contributed to the establishment of its foundations, reveals that, as Peirce alleged, the universe is indeed perfused and virtually made up entirely of signs, among which "man" is one.

To sum up the relation between the signs of the universe and the human being as sign, I propose this formula: "man" is an interpretant whose ideas are signs, having the universe in its totality as their object.

RETROSPECT: HISTORY AND THEORY IN SEMIOTICS

A. THEORY OF SEMIOTICS

The object or subject matter of semiotic inquiry is not just signs but the action of signs or *semiosis*. This action, we now see, occurs at a number of levels that can be distinguished or identified as specific spheres or zones of sign activity.

Semiotics, therefore, contrasts with semiosis as knowledge contrasts with that which is known. Semiotics is knowledge about semiosis; it is the theoretical accounting for signs and what they do.

This is actually an important distinction, because, if we are right in what we have said about the extent of semiosis, the history of semiosis and the history of the universe, at least insofar as the universe inclines toward a species of our linguistic type as part of itself, are the same thing. But the history of *semiotics*, by contrast, is quite another matter and, while complicated, is considerably more manageable. It will be the story of the attempts, more or less fitful, to take account of that which underlies semiosis and makes it possible, namely, the sign. What is a sign such that it makes possible semiosis?

This is the foundational question of semiotic inquiry, the basic question, to which we have essayed an answer in chapter 4, and for which the preceding and following chapters may be regarded as supporting amplifications. Beyond the scope of this book, however, over and above this question, there is the investigation of the role of signs in particular spheres, such as architecture, the fine arts, literature, the codes of dress, legal codes, heraldry, prognostics or symptomatology in medicine, linguistics, historiography, geography, geology, ecosystems, astronomy, chemistry, physics, etc.

But these specialized inquiries into signs of this or that type, the actions of signs in creating and molding this or that objective sphere of experience, oddly enough, have heretofore been normally pursued apart from any thematic consciousness of what a sign is in its distinctive objectivity, of what is distinctive about the objectivity of the sign.

Semiotics thus is the attempt to account theoretically for what is distinctive about the sign, both in its being and in the temporally coterminous action that follows upon that being, according to the ancient saying that "as a being is, so does it act" (*agere sequitur esse*). To the extent that such a reflexive attempt comes to permeate specialized investigations about signs, the reflection imparts to those investigations—no matter how well established and "traditional"—its own thematic unity and assimilates them to the field of investigations properly called "semiotic". Thus, "the field of investigations properly called semiotic" includes *by right* all the traditional disciplines in virtue of their dependency in what they are as typically distinct structures of signification upon a network of sign relations constituting them; but *in fact* the field includes those disciplines only at the moment when and to the extent that, besides being seen to be structures of signification, they are looked at and analyzed thematically in terms of this virtually semiotic constitution. The field of investigations virtually semiotic is coextensive with the field of all investigations, but the actual field of semiotic investigations properly so-called is much smaller at any given moment. It exists as a demand of the future on present thought, in the form, like knowledge itself, of a task being completed rather than of a task done. It finds itself at every moment, to borrow a description from Peirce (1868: 5.316), "dependent on the future thought of the community".

In this way, the history and the theory of semiotics intertwine and grow together. But there is also a certain reflective moment, or series of moments, more or less critical, anterior to which *semiotics* properly speaking, in its contrast with semiosis, does not exist or exists in a very febrile condition.

The history of semiotics in this manner is always twofold. It is first of all a gathering together and identification of those moments of self-consciousness about the sign when signs are not only used but recognized in their contrast with what they are used for. That is to say, semiotics must first, in order to achieve its history, identify and hierarchize those moments where the sign comes to be *recognized* for the role it plays in its own right and not just *deployed* quasi-invisibly in dealings with objects.

Then, retrenching the thematic consciousness thus attained, semiotics as a moment of consciousness expands outward over the whole realm of knowledge and belief to elicit from within each of the disciplines objectively constituted an actual awareness, more or less reluctant, of the semioses and semiotic processes virtually present within them by their very nature as finite knowledge.

In this way, the traditionally established disciplines become themselves transformed semiotically, by being brought to a higher level of self-consciousness and, at the same time, a lower level of isolation within the community of inquirers. This is what is meant by the inherent interdisciplinarity of semiotics, and how semiotics tends to function as an antidote for overspecialization, by imposing an objective awareness of the common processes of signification on which the most specialized achievements of knowledge depend.

This is the expansion of semiotic consciousness along, so to say, the axis of synchronicity.

But the expansion of semiotic consciousness also transpires, and by the same impetus, diachronically, so to say, back across time, over the previous epochs of civilization, art, science, and philosophy, for example, or literature and theology, in order to rethink them and reconsider their products precisely from a semiotic point of view. In this way, semiotics brings about a rewriting of previous thought and consequently of history.

We see, then, that, synchronically and diachronically, the theory of semiotics and the history of semiotics are of a piece, mutually self-constituting. Unlike a natural history, say, of the continents of earth or of the Pterodactyl among the dinosaurs, the object of semiotic history is not actually given until and unless the theory that makes it visible—that is, the consciousness of the sign in its distinctive being—has already been achieved.

The history of semiotics is first of all an achievement of semiotic consciousness and then the working out of the implications of that consciousness, so far as it is able to sustain itself systematically, in every sphere of knowledge and experience. In this way, it is a history that extends also into the future, and will never be completed while thought itself continues to grow.

"Semiotic consciousness" is nothing more nor less than the explicit awareness of the role of the sign as that role is played in a given respect. Since, however, it turns out that the whole of experience, from its origins in sense to its highest achievements of understanding, is constituted by signs, it follows that the history of semiotics will be first of all a tracing of the lines which lead to that moment when this total or comprehensive role of the sign in the constituting of experience and knowledge came to be realized. After that, the history of semiotics will be the working out of the implications of this realization both synchronically and diachronically.

But "diachrony", in this case, is not just a matter of retrospect, or of a sequence of discrete synchronic sections arranged as prior and posterior. The diachrony of semiotic consciousness is the formation of future thought as well as the transmission and comparison of past thought. It involves an awareness of demands the future makes on present thinking in order for present thought to be what it is as containing also what no longer is or might never have been in relation to what could be. In a word, the axes of diachrony and synchrony in semiotic consciousness mark the labile intersection where the critical control of objectivity—"criticism" in the broadest sense—is exercised through the subjectivity of the individual linguistic animal.

Thus, when we speak of the "history" of semiotics, we are obliged to have in mind the working out and rendering publicly accessible, from within the myriad subjectivities of the knowers capable of raising semiosis to the semiotic level, of the implications of the realization of the sign's comprehensive role in the constituting and development of experience diachronically in both directions. It is for this reason that the future of thought, as well as its past, will be different as a result of the achievement of a semiotic consciousness, different, too, in unpredictable ways (because of the factor of chance both in itself and as subjectively diffracted in social life).

In a word, the theory of semiotics in the basic sense will be the explanation of how the whole of knowledge and experience depends on signs, or is a product of semiosis; the history of semiotics in the basic sense will be the tracing of the lines that made such an explanation possible and necessary, even though this history in another sense remains open by virtue of thought in the present to an indefinite future as well.

B. History of Semiotics

Nonetheless, however incomplete it must be prospectively considered, on its retrospective side such a history cannot remain indefinite. It will consist in answering the question: Where was a consciousness of the role of the sign in the totality of human experience thematically and systematically articulated?

Secondarily, such a history will consist in the record of the workings out of the implications of such a consciousness. It will be enough, in keeping with the purpose of the present work, to restrict ourselves to a preliminary answer in outline to the first question: Where in fact was semiotic consciousness first achieved in its integrity?

The answer to that question, simply put, is that semiotic consciousness found its original thematic statement and systematic formulation in the Latin world as it developed indigenously (after the collapse of Rome, which remained dominated in its speculative consciousness by the Greek philosophies and language) between Augustine thematically (c.397AD) and Poinsot systematically (1632). Precisely this development received its name unwittingly from an Englishman, John Locke, in 1690, who suggested in the form of a hypothetical alternative to the perspective in which his own labors had mainly developed a perspective whose development would destroy the speculative substance of those earlier labors, along with the whole subsequent modern development in continuity with them. Finally, in nominal continuity with Locke and speculative continuity with the largely unknown Latin forebears, the range and complexity in detail of the issues that need to be clarified in the perspective of semiotic was illustrated relentlessly in the writings of Charles Sanders Peirce, from his discovery of the semiotic categories, subsuming the concerns of realism and idealism through their common dependency on experience, in 1867, to his death in 1914.

Having tried, for several chapters now, to examine directly the subject matter thus uncovered, let us next try—as befits the self-consciousness the sign imposes through its inescapable lesson of the historicity of thought—to look also historically at what has been examined.

1. The Ancient World and Augustine

Augustine seems to have been the first thinker to have enunciated the idea of *signum* as the universal instrument or means whereby communication of whatever sort and at whatever level is effected. This is a surprising fact, to which too little attention has so far been paid. There is nothing in the world either of ancient Greek philosophy or of the Roman era dominated by this philosophy that corresponds to the notion of "sign" as we have today come to take it for granted, as providing through its distinctive type of action (semiosis) the unified subject matter or object of semiotic inquiry.

The "seme-" root of our term semiotics and its many congeners, of course, is definitively Greek in extraction. But, in the Greek writings extant for us today, the dominant feature in this regard is the split, verging on dichotomic, between *Semēion*/Nature, on the one hand, and *Symbolon*/Culture, on the other hand. This is true of Plato in the *Cratylus* (c.385BC), of Aristotle throughout his works (including notably the woefully mistranslated *Perihermenias* [c.330BC: 16–20a; cf. Eco et al. 1986: 66–68], whereby Boethius [esp. inter 511–513AD] unwittingly increased the impetus of Augustine's suggestions for a unified *doctrina signorum*), and of Greek medicine, which Sebeok (1985: 181) regards (after "linguistic affinities" and "the profoundest strata of human wisdom" conventionally fossilized as philosophical analysis) as "the third, admittedly uneven leg upon which semiotics rests". For, in medicine, it is definitely the semēion/nature side that dominates prognostics (see Sebeok 1984c), despite the "sop to Cerberus" all its own that medicine even today regularly proffers in the placebo—but without by any means being the whole of the story (as is best seen today through the work of Baer 1982, 1988).

Apart from these great icons of ancient Greece, there are also the Stoics, who, in their debates with the Epicureans, unquestionably developed at greatest length the theory of signs in the ancient world but who unfortunately have survived only in fragments conveyed principally by their enemies, Sextus Empiricus (c.200) in particular. General accounts of the Stoic sign theory, more or less comprehensive under the circumstances, can be found in Savan 1986 and 1986a, Eco 1980, and Verbeke 1978. Like the apple of Tantalus, the Stoic writings are there to be enjoyed, if only they could be reached—which makes their allure all the greater. Perhaps this is why a leading expert today on Stoic logic (Mates) routinely imposes upon his exposition of supposedly Stoic conceptions terminology drawn from the framework of symbolic logic after Russell and the early Wittgenstein, while the most fascinating author of abductions on Stoic semiotics (Eco) has turned lately to novels. Clarke's "History of Semiotic" (1987: 12–42) provides an excellent summary here where the evidence is scanty, but after Augustine becomes a phantasmagoric montage constructed of secondary sources standard in traditional philosophy, but based entirely on pre-semiotic research interests.

Augustine's role against the ancient Greek and Roman background has been nicely captured in a recent descriptive summary jointly essayed by Eco, Lambertini, Marmo, and Tabarroni (1986: 65–66):

> It was Augustine who first proposed a 'general semiotics'—that is, a general 'science' or 'doctrine' of signs, where signs become the genus of which words (*onomata*) and natural symptoms (*sēmeîa*) are alike equally species.
>
> Medieval semiotics knows at this point two lines of thinking as possibly unified, but without having achieved their actual unification. . . . Out of the tension of this opposition—under the provocation, as it were, of Augustine—is born much of the distinctively Latin development of semiotic consciousness.

Echoes of the tension persist to this day, as in Husserl's quintessentially modern and at the same time contemporary attempt to deny the possible unity of a semiotic consciousness (cf. Kruse 1986), or more generally throughout the academic world, as evidenced in Eco (1982) and in the ongoing "nature/nurture" controversy in psychology and anthropology.

2. The Latin World

If we measure the development of semiotic consciousness in terms of the resolution of this tension in favor of the possible unity Augustine originally glimpsed, then the main lines of this development occur after William of Ockham (i.1317–1328), paradoxically, in the resistance of the logicians, first at Paris and later at Coimbra and Alcalá, to the acceptance of Augustine's proffered definition of the sign. Although general far beyond notions found in the ancient world, nonetheless, as in the ancient world, Augustine's definition envisioned for every sign a necessary linkage of a sensible element or vehicle with a possibly immaterial—that is, as such imperceptible—content signified.

The objection of the logicians concerned precisely what John Locke would shortly (1690) see as the first task confronting the would-be semiotician, namely, the bringing of outward signs such as words and gestures and the interior means of knowing such as images and ideas under the common perspective afforded by the notion of sign.

The origins of this rebellion against the age-old linkage of signs with the sense-perceptible are as yet obscure but seem definitely linked to the influence of Ockham at Paris and his introduction of the notion of the concept as a "signum naturale". Clearly afoot as early as Petrus d'Ailly (c.1372) was the further designation of the interior means of knowing as "signa formalia", contrasting with the outward "signa instrumentalia" whereby the known or felt inwardly is shared publicly. Williams (1985a: xxxiii) made the following summary of the historical situation in this regard:

> A major strand of semiotic reflection and controversy, beginning from at least the fourteenth century and developing especially in the Iberian university world of the sixteenth and seventeenth centuries, but involving also a wide geographic area . . . turned precisely on this question of whether the sign as such involves a *per se* sensible half. The increasingly consistent answer was made in the negative.
>
> But what is of principal interest here is that, as it turns out, this point of historical controversy is the central point theoretically for the accomplishment of the main task of semiotic as Locke proposed it, to wit, the bringing of ideas as well as words into the perspective of a doctrine of signs.

3. The Iberian Connection

The transition figure in establishing an Iberian connection for this revolutionary underground of high medieval semiotics was Dominicus Soto. His early studies at Paris led him to introduce into the Iberian milieu (1529, 1554) an *ad hoc* series of distinctions effectively conveying the objection to the linkage of signs as such (that is, in their essential being and consequent active function in experience) to the sensible vehicle as sign. This had the effect of forcing the issues of the dependency of objectivity throughout on sign functions, and therefore of a sign function that is presupposed to the level of what can be observed and experienced directly as an object. I give first Williams' summary of the central issues and then resume briefly the historical lines of reaction to them (Williams 1985a: xxxi-xxxii):

> What actually is common to *all* treatments of the sign, from ancient times to the present, [is,] namely, the seeing of the sign as a 'mask of Janus', bi-facial, or 'relative to the cognitive powers of some organism, on the one hand, and to the content signified on the other'. If it is therefore this *relativity* that constitutes the being proper to signs, then why . . . add the further condition that this relativity has to be grounded in an object of sense as such?
>
> It is precisely the inclusion as essential of this further condition which is not essential . . . which has inevitably confused the discussion of the nature or being proper to signs—'all signs insofar as they are signs'. The crux of the problem concerns the 'difference between a sign functioning as such *from within* the cognitive powers of an organism, and a sign functioning as such by impacting on those powers *from without*'. This difference [is] crucial to the functioning of signs . . . insofar as the ground of observability in the perceiver, or that which makes him or her be a perceiver, is not as such itself susceptible of observation.
>
> It follows . . . that the taking into account of this distinction gives rise to 'the true ground question' for a doctrine of signs: 'In what does the relativity essential to signifying properly consist?' This question . . . has never been resolved satisfactorily *within* specifically realist or idealist paradigms of thought. . . . The breakthrough resolution of John Poinsot in his *Treatise on Signs* (1632a) was itself anomalous in terms of previous traditions as well as in terms of what it anticipated. In contrast, pre-semiotic realist or idealist paradigms of thought have failed, respectively, either to appreciate that perception itself structures its object as relative, or to appreciate that ideas are signs *before becoming objects* of our awareness, and, as signs, can give access to 'the nature of things' (to nature, that is) only as revealed *relatively* through signs.

Two major reactions to these issues appeared at Coimbra. One favored, in effect, restoring the ancient perspective (Fonseca 1564). The other promoted rather the prospective unity heralded by Augustine (the Conimbricenses 1607), but without being able to show finally *how* the being of signs provides a purchase for such an over-all perspective.

The decisive development in this regard was the privileged achievement of John Poinsot, a student with the Conimbricenses, and the successor, after a century, to Soto's own teaching position at the University of Alcalá de Henares. With a single stroke of genius resolving the controversies, since Boethius, over the interpretation of relative being in the categorial scheme of Aristotle, Poinsot (1632a 117/28–118/18, esp. 118/14–18, annotated in Deely 1985: 472–479) was able to provide semiotics with a unified object conveying the action of signs both in nature virtually and in experience actually, as at work at all three of the analytically distinguishable levels of conscious life (sensation, perception, intellection). By this same stroke he was also able to reconcile in the univocity of the object signified the profound difference between what is and what is not either present in experience here and now or present in physical nature at all (Poinsot 1632a: Book III).

Poinsot was able to reduce to systematic unity Soto's *ad hoc* series of distinctions, as he put it in his first announcement of the work of his *Treatise* ("Lectori", 1631; p. 5 of the Deely 1985 edition), and thereby to complete the gestation in Latin philosophy of the first foundational treatise establishing the fundamental character of, and the ultimate simplicity of the standpoint determining, the issues that govern the unity and scope of the doctrine of signs. Unfortunately, because he so skillfully embedded his *Tractatus de Signis* within a massive and traditional Aristotelian *cursus philosophiae naturalis*, he unwittingly ensured its slippage into oblivion in the wake of Descartes' modern revolution. Three hundred and six years would pass between the original publication of Poinsot's *Treatise on Signs* and the first frail appearance of some of its leading ideas in late modern culture (Maritain 1937–1938, discussed in Deely 1986d).

4. The Place of John Locke

Coincidentally, Poinsot achieved his Herculean labor of the centuries in the birth year of the man whose privilege it would be, while knowing nothing of Poinsot's work, to give the perspective so achieved what was to become its proper name. Thus, 1632 was both the year John Locke was born and the year that Poinsot's treatise on signs was published. The name-to-be for what both Locke and Poinsot and, later Peirce also, called "the doctrine of signs"—an expression of pregnant import in its own right, as Sebeok (1976a: ix) was first to notice (elaborated in Deely 1978a, 1982b, 1986b *inter alia*)—was proposed publicly fifty-eight years later, in 1690, in the five closing paragraphs (little more than the very last page) of Locke's *Essay concerning Humane Understanding*.

The principal instigation that Locke himself wrote in reaction against, but along very different lines from what he would end by proposing for "semiotic", was the Cartesian attempt (1637, 1641) to claim for rational thought a complete separation from any dependency on sensory experience.

The irony of the situation in this regard was that Locke's principal objections to Descartes were not at all furthered by the speculative course he set at the beginning and pursued through the body of his monumental *Essay concerning Humane Understanding* of 1690. Instead, he furthered the Cartesian revolution in spite of himself; deflected the brilliant suspicions of Berkeley (1732); fathered the cynical skepticism of Hume (1748);[47] and laid

---

47. Miller (1979) makes a strong argument in fact that Hume's skepticism was rooted in a

the seeds of overthrow of his own work in concluding it with the suggestion that what is really needed is a complete reconsideration of "*Ideas* and *Words*, as the great Instruments of Knowledge" in the perspective that a doctrine of signs would make possible. The consideration of the means of knowing and communicating within the perspective of signifying, he presciently suggested, "would afford us another sort of Logick and Critick, than what we have hitherto been acquainted with". It was for this possible development that he proposed the name *semiotic*.

The antinomy between the actual point of view adopted at the beginning for the *Essay* as a whole and the possible point of view proposed at its conclusion (Deely 1986a) is, for semiotic historiography, an object worthy of consideration in its own right.

It remains that to Locke goes the privilege and power of the naming. If today we call the doctrine of signs "semiotic" and not "semiology", it is to the brief concluding chapter XX in the original edition of Locke's *Essay* that we must look for the reason—there, and to the influence this chapter exercised on the young American thinker, Charles Sanders Peirce, who read the *Essay* but made of its conclusion a substantial part of his philosophy and lifework from 1867 onward.

5. Ferdinand de Saussure, Charles S. Peirce, and John Poinsot

Contemporaneously with Peirce, and independently both of him and of Locke, Ferdinand de Saussure was also suggesting that the doctrine of signs was a development whose time had come. For this development he proposed a name (i.1911–1916: 33):

> We shall call it *sēmíology* (from the Greek sēmeîon, 'sign'). It would teach us what signs consist of and what laws govern them.

While recognizing that, inasmuch as "it does not yet exist, one cannot say what form it will take", Saussure wished to insist that the prospective science in question is one that "has a right to existence" and a place "marked out in advance". It will study "the life of signs at the heart of so-

---

kind of radically vitiated semiotic wherein the content of experience was reduced to the skein of its structure. Hume, "for reasons of his own, fails to make explicit", Miller avers (p. 43), "that the causal relation, as he describes it, is essentially what the philosophical tradition had understood as a sign relation". Along this line, Miller is able to suggest a semiotic interpretation for the British tradition as a whole "between the mid-seventeenth and the mid-eighteenth centuries" (p. 51): "the relation of cause and effect is reduced to what previously had been understood as a sign relationship", but without ever having been radically thought through in what is proper to it or clarified in its ground. On this interpretation, modern idealism itself would have been a consequence of the failure of modern philosophers to explore the semiotic option Locke called for belatedly and little-noticed.

cial life" and be "a branch of social psychology". "The laws that semiology will discover" are, accordingly, the laws governing "the totality of human phenomena", or culture in its contrast with nature.

We see then that Saussure's intuition was fatally flawed in its original formulation. He placed on his intuition of the need for a science of signs the fatal qualification of viewing it as a subordinate (or "subaltern") rather than as an architectonic discipline respecting the whole of human belief, knowledge, and experience, as we have seen its internal requirements dictate. He further compromised his proposal for the enterprise by making of linguistics "le patron générale de toute sémiologie", raising the "arbitrariness of signs" into a principle of analysis for all expressive systems. Thereby he obscured the much more fundamental interplay of the subjectivity of the physical environment and the subjectivity of the cognizing organism in the constitution of objectivity for *Umwelten* in general and the human *Lebenswelt* in particular, whereby, in the latter case, even the linguistic sign in its public functioning becomes assimilated from the start to a natural form, as far as its users are concerned.

The duality of *signifiant* and *signifié*, in a word, lacked the thirdness whereby the sign in its foundation (and whether or not this foundation be essentially arbitrary or "stipulated") undergoes transformation into first an object and then into other signs. The dynamics of the process linking semiosis in culture with semiosis in nature, and making one the extension of the other in an ongoing spiral of interactions, needs to be brought in. But, for that, the framework needs to be radically reformulated. As far as the contemporary establishment of semiotics goes, it was the privilege of Charles Sanders Peirce to provide just such an alternative framework under the influence of Locke's suggestion.

Let us look with some care at what Peirce did with Locke's suggestion, and see if we can see with something of dispassion "Why", as Short put it (1988), "we prefer Peirce to Saussure" today. We will see at the same time something of the doctrinal convergence Peirce, working with contemporary and modern materials, achieves with the foundational synthesis of a doctrine of signs distillated by Poinsot from the materials of Greek antiquity and the Latin middle age.

Beginning with his "New List of Categories" in 1867, and continuing until his death in 1914, semiotic in this broadest sense of the study of semiosis surrounding, as well as within, the human world provided the thrust underlying and the unity for a substantial part, and perhaps even for the whole, of Peirce's philosophy.[48]

---

48. The centrality of semiotic was something which came to be realized only gradually, and by later students of Peirce's thought. Only gradually were the perceptions imposed by the pre-established perspectives brought to the study of Peirce's own thought (such as realism, idealism, and, in particular, "pragmatism", to name a few) overcome, by the requirements of the thought itself. Arguably, it is as an effect of this situation in particular that all of the

At the same time, even in the "New List of Categories" as originally drafted, it is fair to say that Peirce labored overly under the influence of Kant as Master of the Moderns—that is to say, between the horns of the dilemma set by the (false) dichotomy of the realism versus idealism controversy. Since, as I think, semiotic in principle and by right—the *jus signi*, let us say—begins by transcending the terms of this controversy, it is not surprising that Peirce had such a time of it whenever he succumbed to the temptation to try to classify his own work in realist-idealist terms. Assuming naturally the terms of the controversy as it had developed over the course of modern thought, he only gradually came to critical terms with the fact that semiotic as such is a form neither of realism nor of idealism, but beyond both.

As a disciple of Kant in early life, Peirce labored at the impossible task of establishing the complete autonomy of the ideal/mental from what is individually existent in nature. In later life he concluded that this erroneous quest had vitiated modern philosophy (1903: 1.19–21). Significant of this evolution of his thought is the fact that in Peirce's later philosophy his supreme category of Thirdness changed from representation in 1867 to triadic relation as common to both representations and to laws existent in nature (c.1899: 1.565).

By his Lowell Lectures of 1903, and even already in his c.1890 "Guess at the Riddle", it is clear that Peirce was well on the way to taking his categories of semiosis properly in hand and was marking out a course of future development for philosophy (as semiotic) that is nothing less than a new age, as different in its characteristics as is the "realism" of Greek and Latin times from the idealism of modern times in the national languages.

In his "Minute Logic" (c.1902a: 1.203–272) we have a lengthy analysis of what he calls "ideal" or "final" causality. He assimilates these two terms as descriptions of the same general type of causality (ibid.: 1.211, 227). But, in successive analyses (ibid.: 1.211, 214, 227, 231; and similarly in 1903: 1.26), it emerges that causality by ideas constitutes the more general form of this sort of explanation, inasmuch as final causality, being concerned with mind, purpose, or quasi-purpose, is restricted to psychology and biol-

---

earlier publications concerning Peirce, including notably the *Collected Papers*, have been relegated to the status of provisional enterprises.

But it may also be (see particularly Kent 1987), as suggested in his breakdown of philosophy into Phenomenology (the categories), Normative Science (esthetics, ethics, and semiotics), and Metaphysics (first philosophy), that Peirce himself did not finally realize how radical semiotics is as a form of knowledge vis-à-vis the established disciplines ("First Philosophy" in particular, as I have pointed out in 1987 and 1988a), in which case he remains in this particular *primus inter pares* among the moderns in view of semiotics, rather than, as I think (for example, see c.1909: 6.322), the contemporary *pater semioticorum*.

Given the complexity of the Peircean writings and the increasing interest in their exegesis, we may safely leave this question for future resolution by the exegetes. Our interest here is not in anyone's texts as such, but in the basics of semiotics, as we have said.

ogy (c.1902a: 1.269), whereas ideal causality in its general type requires as such neither purpose (1.211) nor mind nor soul (1.216: cf. the analysis of Poinsot 1632a: 177/8–178/7).

Now Peirce identifies this ideal causality with his category of Thirdness, the central element of his semiotic (1903: 1.26) and the locus for any account of narrative, or of "lawfulness of any kind". Thirdness consists of triadic relations (c.1899: 1.565). In these triadic relations the foundations specify the several relations in different ways, so that one relation is specified, for example, as "lover of", and another as "loved by" (1897: 3.466).

Thanks to their specification, triadic relations have a certain generality (c.1902a: 2.92; 1903: 1.26). Signs constitute one general class of triadic relations, and the laws of nature (which are expressed through signs) constitute the other general class (c.1896: 1.480). Signs themselves are either genuine or degenerate. Genuine signs concern existential relations between interacting bodies and need an interpretant to be fully specified as signs (c.1902a: 2.92). For the genuine triadic sign relation is a mind-dependent similarity relation between the object of the existential relation and the existential relation itself as object for the interpretant (1904: 8.332). For example, words need an interpretant to be fully specified as signs. Triadic sign relations that are degenerate in the first degree concern existential relations between interacting bodies but require no interpretant to make them fully specified as signs. For example, a rap on the door means a visitor, with no explanation needed. Triadic sign relations that are degenerate in the second degree concern mind-dependent relations specified by the intrinsic possibility of the objects with which they are concerned, because these relations cannot vary between truth and falsity whatever any human group may think, as for example, in the case of mathematics, logic, ethics, esthetics, psychology, and poetry (1903a: 5.125; 1908: 6.455; c.1909: 6.328).

It is clear that when either science or literature, or anything in between, is considered in a semiotic framework as comprehensive as this, an exclusive treatment of its processes from the standpoint of constructed signs simply will not do. We risk being lost in crossword puzzles of great interest, maybe, but without validity as modes of understanding the semiosis peculiar to humanity as it extends and links up again with the semiosis that weaves together human beings with the rest of life and nature.

Thus, the work of Peirce is regarded justly as the greatest achievement of any American philosopher, and at the same time the emergence of semiotic as the major tradition of intellectual life today throws the lost work of Poinsot into relief for its original contribution. Just as the writings of the American philosopher Charles Peirce first illustrated something of the comprehensive scope and complexity in detail of issues that need to be clarified and thought through anew in the perspective of semiotic, so did the Iberian *Tractatus de Signis* of John Poinsot first express the fundamental character of these issues in light of the ultimate simplicity of the standpoint determining the semiotic point of view. The Dean of Peirce scholarship, Max H. Fisch, comments with emphasis in this regard (1986) that, within its limits, Poinsot's work provides us with "the most *systematic* treatise on signs that has ever been written".

Just as semiotics itself appears today as a completely unexpected development within the traditionally established entrenchments of disciplinary specialization, so does it require a thorough re-examination of the relation of modern thought in its mainstream development to Latin times in general and to the Iberian Latin development in particular. In renewing the history of thought and restoring unity to the ancient enterprise of so-called philosophical understanding, Poinsot's work occupies a privileged position in the mainstream of semiotic discourse as we see it developing today. "Poinsot's thought", Sebeok points out (1982: x),

> belongs decisively to that mainstream as the 'missing link' between the ancients and the moderns in the history of semiotic, a pivot as well as a divide between two huge intellective landscapes the ecology of neither of which could be fully appreciated prior to this major publishing event.

For the fundamental reason pointed out by Williams (1987a: 480) in observing "that historical narrative is the only logic capable of situating competing traditions and incommensurate paradigms in a perspective that not only lends each a higher degree of clarity on its own terms as well as in relation to the others, but also decides which paradigms will emerge as victorious", the perspective of semiotic requires of anyone seeking to adopt and develop it a cultivation also of a sense of how the transmissibility of the past in anthroposemiosis is an essential constituent and not something at the margins of present consciousness.

In this way, in particular, semiotics puts an end, long overdue, to the Cartesian revolution (the collection edited by Chenu 1984 is very helpful in this regard) and to the pretensions of scientific thought to transcend, through mathematical means, the human condition. The model for semiotics is rather that of a community of inquirers, precisely because "the human *Umwelt* presents us with a continuum of past, present, and future in which continuity and change, convention and invention, commingle, and of which the ultimate source of unity is *time*" (Williams 1985: 274). Thus, the work of Williams (1982, 1983, 1984, 1985–1987, 1987a, 1988) and of Pencak (1987; Williams and Pencak, forthcoming) in penetrating the traditional field of historiographical study from an explicitly semiotic point of view, is one of the most essential advances in the developing understanding of semiotics today.

Eventually, we will see that the doctrine of signs requires for its full possibilities a treating of history as the laboratory within which semiosis, anthroposemiosis in particular, achieves its results, and to which it must constantly recur when an impasse is reached or new alternatives are required. Thirdness, after all, is what history is all about.

6. *Jakob von Uexküll*

So far, we have seen that the small number of pioneers—in particular, Poinsot, Peirce, and, to a lesser extent, Saussure—who tried to explore and establish directly the foundational concepts for a doctrine of signs found the way clogged with an underbrush of conceptual difficulties rooted in the prevailing thought structures and obstructing the access to the vantage point from which the full expanse of semiotic might be developed. Peirce, for this reason (c.1907a: 5.488), described the pioneer work "of clearing and opening up" *semiotic* as the task rather of a *backwoodsman*.

Once the foundations have been secured, there remains the task of building the edifice and the enterprise of semiotic understanding, by elucidating at all points the crucial processes comprising the interface of nature and culture summed up in the term *semiosis*. This task, too, is clogged by underbrush accruing from presemiotic thought structures that must be cut away as semiotics reclaims from previous thought contributions essential to its own enterprise of reflective understanding.

We have now to see how the history and theory of semiotics includes as well background figures who, without explicitly understanding their work as semiotic, have made useful and even decisive contributions toward the recognition of what appears in its full propriety within the widening vista of semiotics. In the case of thinkers who did not deal directly, in the sense of with set and conscious purpose, with the notion of semiotic foundations, the wrestling in areas of semiosic functionings with conceptual difficulties accruing from obstructive thought structures is made all the more difficult for the want of an explicit entertainment of an alternative to the prevailing mindsets. In such a case, the very obstructions risk being incorporated into the creative conceptions themselves. When this happens, an inevitable degree of distortion results, to the extent that the creative novelties become assimilated to paradigms exclusive of the foundational clarity and expanse the perspective of semiotics could eventually provide.

There are thus three classes of what Rauch (1983) calls semiotists: there are the semioticians, workers who begin from the vantage point and within the perspective of the sign; there are the pioneers or founding figures of semiotics, the protosemioticians, who struggled to establish the essential nature and fundamental varieties of possible semiosis; and there are also, among the ranks of present and past workers of the mind, cryptosemioticians, who need themselves to become aware of the perspective that semiotic affords[49] or whose work needs to be by others reclaimed and re-established from within that perspective.[50] In particular, oppositions seemingly irreconcilable from the standpoint of the customary juxtaposition of idealism to realism often admit of subsumption within a higher synthesis from the vantage of semiotic. In such a way, apparent contradictions within the history of semiotics need not always remain so at the level of theory.

Here, and by way of concluding our historical sketch, we will deal with the case of one of the greatest cryptosemioticians of the century immediately following the publication in 1867 of Peirce's "New List of Categories", Jakob von Uexküll. The *Umwelt-Forschung* he pioneered (1899–1940) is probably the most important recent illustration of a cryptosemiotic enterprise transcending, in the direction of semiotic, the limitations it otherwise imposed upon itself by embracing too intimately the mindset and paradigm immediately available in the milieu of the time and place.

When we talk of the Umwelt, as we have seen, we are talking about the central category of zoösemiosis and anthroposemiosis alike. The objective world generated at only these levels of semiosis finally constitutes, to borrow Toews's felicitous phrase (1987), "the autonomy of meaning and the irreducibility of experience" to anything that might be supposed to exist independently of it. This concept, belonging to the biological foundations that "lie at the very epicenter of the study of both communication and signification in the human animal" (Sebeok 1976a: x), we owe principally to the work of Jakob von Uexküll. So it is not surprising that von Uexküll has begun to emerge within contemporary semiotics as perhaps the single most important background thinker for understanding the biological conditions of our experience of the world in the terms required by semiotic.[51]

---

49. As happened in the case of Harley Shands in the context of medicine, or more recently to Martin Esslin in the context of drama, according to his own report (1987: 10): "This *semiotic* approach is, basically, extremely simple and practical. It asks: how is it done? and tries to supply the most down-to-earth answers, by examining the *signs* that are used to achieve the desired communication.

"There is, of course, nothing radically new here, except that the enterprise is systematic and methodical rather than ad-hoc and impressionistic. When I first came across the beginnings of the new scholarly literature on the *semiology* and *semiotics* of the theatre and film I felt rather like Molière's M. Jourdain who was surprised to discover that he had been talking 'prose' all his life."

50. Of the two alternatives, the first is preferable by far, but it is available only to present and future workers, just as this second alternative is the only one available in the task of bringing within the perspective of semiotic works whose creators belong irrevocably to the past. The second alternative defines the requirements of semiotic historiography, which has, as one among its several tasks, to "assess the contributions of a host of 'neglected' giants". It was in this context that Sebeok (1976a: x) coined the term "cryptosemiotician".

51. In this respect, Jakob von Uexküll's role in semiotics has some important structural isomorphisms with the role of Frege in the development of analytic philosophy or of Brentano in the development of phenomenology (see Deely 1975).

Having already shown synchronically how useful this concept is to semiotics, we will now look at von Uexküll's work diachronically in terms of its "semiotic lag", the phenomenon wherein the terms used in articulating a newer, developing paradigm inevitably reflect the older ways of thinking in contrast to which the new development is taking place, and hence constitute a kind of drag on the development, until a point is reached whereat it becomes possible to coin effectively a fresh turn of phrase reflecting precisely the new rather than the old. The new terminology has the simultaneous effect of ceasing the drag and highlighting what in fact was developing all along (cf. Merrell 1987).

In the case of Jakob von Uexküll, the drag is a consequence of having rooted his biological theories to an eventually counterproductive degree in the philosophy of Immanuel Kant (1781, 1787). On the positive side, it was Kant who best focussed thematic attention on the constructive regularities at work from the side of the subject in establishing the objects of experience so far as they belong to the phenomenal realm of the appearances of everyday life. Appreciation of the constructive role of the cognitive powers of the knowing subject and of that subject's affective shaping of cognitive content in the presentation through perception of what is known was, to be sure, an essential advance of philosophical understanding in the matter of dealing theoretically with the origins of knowledge and the nature of experience in the assessments of belief and practices. The emphasis on these matters communicated from Kant to von Uexküll was indispensable.

Dispensable was the Kantian failure to deal with the rationale according to which the constructive elements contributed by the subject—so-called concepts or ideas—are abductively arrived at as necessary postulates in the first place. This rationale was one of the several threads in the discussions crucial for epistemology that developed over the closing Latin centuries—particularly in Iberia—and were lost to the modern development as it took place, after Descartes, through the Latin filter of Suarez's *Disputationes Metaphysicae* of 1597.

In the German and Kantian context—even more, if possible, than in the modern context generally—the opposition of the terms "subjective" and "objective" is a firmly established dichotomy whose transparency is self-evident. Within this context, von Uexküll himself, who, as his son notes (T. von Uexküll 1981: 148), did not think of his work thematically under the rubric of semiotic, had little alternative to seeing the Umwelt in opposition to the supposed and so-called objective, and as belonging to the phenomenal realm in Kant's sense—on the side of the "subjective", that is, dichotomically conceived in opposition to the supposed "objective".

The want of alternative for von Uexküll himself has resulted in considerable confusion regarding his work in general (through misplaced associations with "vitalism") and, specifically, in notorious difficulties in interpreting (or "translating") the key term, "Umwelt".[52] The difficulties are a clue to the real problem.[53] As far as semiotics is concerned, von Uexküll's work needs to be thought through afresh at the level of basic terminology generally and specifically as regards the extent of reliance placed on the Kantian scheme for philosophy of mind.

T. von Uexküll, for example, in explaining his father's work for the context of semiotics today, unwittingly brings out the inconsistency that obtains between an orthodox Kantian perspective and the perspective of semiotic. According to the son's account (I choose an example where the inconsistency that runs throughout the account is concisely illustrated within one short paragraph, T. von Uexküll 1981: 161): on the one hand, "A schema is a strictly private program" for the formation of complex signs "in our subjective universe"; and, on the other hand, "The schemata which we have formed during our life are intersubjectively identical" at least "in the most general outlines". But, of course, to speak of the intersubjective save as a pure *appearance*, in a Kantian context, is as internally inconsistent as to speak of a grasping of the *Ding-an-sich* in that same context (as Hegel best noted).

The conflict, thus, is between an idealist perspective in which the mind knows only what it constructs and the semiotic perspective in which what the mind constructs and what is partially prejacent to those constructions interweave objectively to constitute indistinctly what is directly experienced and known.

Himself immersed in the Kantian philosophy—that is, the most classi-

---

52. Schiller (1957: xiii), for example, refers to the difficulty of rendering von Uexküll's key terms outside the German–especially Umwelt but also the related terms "by which von Uexküll seeks to represent the relations between the objective world and the world as it appears to the animal". Here, the term "objective" retains entirely its presemiotic content where it is a misleading synonym for the prejacent physical being of the environment, which being, we have seen, is in fact a form of subjectivity, equally with the knower as organism forming part of the physical surroundings. Since she was undertaking her work of translation against this radically presemiotic interpretive horizon, it was fortunate indeed that she decided to retain Umwelt in her translation and to allow the new English context to give this technical term a new sense beyond the explicit choices of a translator. (Perhaps she was sufficiently warned by MacKinnon's "translation" of von Uexküll 1920, which left everything in the dark: better at least to bring one term, the central one, into the light of day!)
53. It is worth asking why, if von Uexküll's key terms within German have only an explicitly Kantian sense, have they been so widely misunderstood also by German speakers who know quite well the Kantian philosophy? Our reappropriation from the modern context of the term "object" and "objective", as deployed in the present work, seems to me necessary to make sense of the very title von Uexküll gives to a main section in one of his key essays (1934: 73), "The Same Subject as an Object in Different Umwelten". In reality, the problem is more doctrinal than linguistic: von Uexküll's terms are also original in German, although their novelty there is hidden behind the pre-existing verbal forms. The problem, as I have recently had occasion to argue at length in relation to other thinkers (Deely 1986e, 1988), is more radical and also systematic. The problem is one of perspective: the perspective of semiotic is not assimilable to the previous perspective of an idealism any more than of a realism.

cal of the classical modern idealisms—Jakob von Uexküll yet was creating in spite of that immersion, through a creative intuition of his own, a notion anticipating another context entirely, a context which had yet to catalyze thematically and receive general acceptance under its own proper name, to wit, the context of semiotic as the doctrine of signs. He was inadvertently precipitating a paradigm shift. A formula I applied to Heidegger (1986: 56), *mutatis mutandis* (that is, substituting "biologist" for "philosopher" and "from within" for "against") can be applied to Jakob von Uexküll: among modern biologists he is the one who struggled most from within the coils of German idealism and in the direction of a semiotic.

For, unlike Heidegger, who expressly wrestled with reaching an alternative to the existing paradigms both realist and idealist, von Uexküll embraced a horn of the false dilemma: he saw himself as merely extending the Kantian paradigm to biology. He did not see that such an "adaptation" presupposed a capacity of human understanding incompatible with the original claims Kant thought to establish for rational life by his initiative. In other words, to apply Kant's paradigm as von Uexküll intended, it was necessary in the application already to transcend the paradigm—an adaptation of the original through mutation indeed.

The genuine adoption by a human observer of the point of view of another life form, on which Umwelt research is predicated, is a-priori impossible in the original Kantian scheme. Either *Umweltensforschung* is a form of transcendental illusion, or, if it is valid—if, for example, von Frisch really did interpret with some correctness the bee's dance or von Uexküll the toad's search image—then von Uexküll, in extending Kant's ideas to biology, was also doing something more, something that the Kantian paradigm did not allow for, namely, achieving objectively and grasping as such an intersubjective correspondence between subjectivities attained through the sign relation.[54]

Once it is understood that the classical terms of the subject-object dichotomy are rendered nugatory within the perspective of a doctrine of signs and that, within this context, the term "objective" functions precisely

54. Von Uexküll's work can be regarded from this point of view as an indirect demonstration, through an inadvertent *reductio*, that the elaborate constructive work that Kant had attributed to human reason as such, first of all and primarily belongs rather to perceptual and sensory apprehension in what of it contrasts essentially with the apprehension distinctive of the understanding which, in its proper act, is constructive secondarily rather than primarily. The primary act of distinctively human intelligence is intuitive, rendered existential through its continuity with sensation, and, at the same time, constructive through its dependence upon perception and species-specific biological heritage as well as past experience. But its primary act in its own order, at each moment, would seem to be to see and *to recognize* within the very constructions of objectivity the problem of other as other—that is, as revealed within the constructions as also more than and aspectually disengageable through analysis from the constructions—whence arise all the further problems of justice on the one hand ("morality") and science on the other. As we saw in chapter 5, it is a question of the sort of apprehension required for objects to possess within experience the extrinsic denomination of stipulability.

to mean the prospectively intersubjective, in opposition to *both* terms of the dichotomy classically understood, new possibilities of understanding are opened up. These possibilities are more in line with what is at the center of, the original to, von Uexküll's work than could be seen through the filter of Kantian idealism, which provided at the time the only developed language available to a scientist of philosophical bent. As "a consistently shared point of view, having as its subject matter all systems of signs irrespective of their substance and without regard to the species of the emitter or receiver involved" (Sebeok 1968: 64), semiotics requires a theoretical foundation equally comprehensive. That foundation can be provided only by an understanding of the being with its consequent causality and action proper to signs in their universal role. With all the subdivisions, neither a perspective of traditional idealism nor of traditional realism has the required expanse.

As semiotics comes of age, it must increasingly free itself from the drag of pre-existing philosophical paradigms. Beginning with the sign—that is, from the function of signs taken in their own right within our experience (semiosis)—it is the task of semiotics to create a new paradigm—its own— and to review, criticize, and improve wherever possible all previous accounts of experience, knowledge and belief in the terms of *that* paradigm. It is thus that the *history* of semiotics and the *theory* of semiotics are only virtually distinct, forming together the actual whole of human understanding as an achievement, a *prise de conscience*, in process and in community.

The maxim for that process, accordingly, is the same as the maxim for semiotics itself: *Nil est in intellectum nec in sensum quod non prius habeatur in signum* ("There is nothing in thought or in sensation which is not first possessed in a sign").[55] For if the *anthropos* as semiotic animal is an interpretant of semiosis in nature and culture alike, that can only be because the ideas of this animal, in their function as signs, are not limited to either order, but have rather, as we explained above, the universe in its totality—"all that wider universe, embracing the universe of existents as a part"—as their object.

---

55. Those interested in the linguistic peculiarities of the maxim's formation grammatically considered should consult the Foreword to the *Semiotics 1987* Annual Proceedings Volume of the Semiotic Society of America, page v in particular.

References

d'AILLY, Pierre.
  c.1372. *Conceptus et Insolubilia*, annotated trans. by Paul Vincent Spade as *Concepts and Insolubles* (Dordrecht, Holland: D. Reidel, 1980).
ANDERSON, Myrdene, John DEELY, Martin KRAMPEN, Joseph RANSDELL, Thomas A. SEBEOK, and Thure von UEXKÜLL.
  1984. *A Semiotic Perspective on the Sciences: Steps Toward a New Paradigm* (Toronto Semiotic Circle Working Paper), since published under the same title as a "position paper" article in *Semiotica* 52–1/2 (1984), 7–47; and, with further refinements, as Chapter 3 of Sebeok 1986a: 17–44 (q.v.), to which final version page references are keyed in this book.
AQUINAS, Thomas.
  c.1252–1256. *Scriptum super libros sententiarum magistri Petri Lombardi*, 4 vols.; vols. 1 and 2 ed. R. P. Mandonnet (Paris: Lethielleux, 1929), vols. 3 and 4 ed. R. P. Maria Fabianus Moos (Paris: Lethielleux, 1939 and 1947).
  c.1265–1267. *Quaestiones Disputatae de Potentia*, ed. Paul M. Pession, in *Quaestiones Disputatae*, vol. II, 9th ed. rev. by P. Biazzi, M. Calcaterra, T. S. Centi, E. Odetto, and P. M. Pession (Turin: Marietti, 1953), 7–276.
  c.1266–1272. *In Aristotelis Librum de Anima Commentarium*, ed. A. M. Pirotta (3rd ed.; Turin: Marietti, 1948).
  c.1269. *In decem libros ethicorum Aristotelis ad Nicomachum expositio*, ed. R. Spiazzi (3rd ed.; Turin: Marietti, 1964).
ARISTOTLE.
  c.335–334BC. *Meteorologica*, trans. E. W. Webster in *The Works of Aristotle*, ed. W. D. Ross (Oxford: The Clarendon Press, 1931), Volume 3.
  c.330BC. *Peri Hermenias*, trans. Boethii *De Interpretatione*, in *Aristoteles Latinus*, Vol. II, parts 1–2, ed. L. Minio-Paluello (Paris: Desclée de Brouwer, 1965); English trans. E. M. Edghill, *On Interpretation*, in McKeon ed. 1941: 38–61.
ATKINS, G. Douglas.
  1981. "The Sign as a Structure of Difference: Derridean Deconstruction and Some of Its Implications", in De George 1981, q.v.
AUGUSTINE.
  c.397–426. *De Doctrina Christiana Libri Quattuor* recensuit et praefatus est Guilelmus M. Green, Vol. LXXX of *Corpus scriptorum ecclesiasticorum Latinorum*, editum consilio et empensis Academiae Scientiarum Austriacae (Vienna: Hoelder-Pichler-Tempsky, 1963); an English trans. by D. W. Robertson, *On Christian Doctrine* (Indianapolis: Bobbs-Merrill, 1977), was consulted.
BAER, Eugen.
  1982. "The Medical Symptom", *The American Journal of Semiotics* 1.3, 17–34; corrected and reprinted in Deely, Williams, and Kruse 1986: 140–152.

1988. *Medical Semiotics. The State of the Art* (= Sources in Semiotics VII; Lanham, MD: University Press of America).

BAKHTIN, Mikhail.

1963. *Problemy poetiki Dostoevskogo* (Moscow), revised and expanded version of *Problemy tvorchestva Dostoevskogo* (Leningrad 1929), trans. as *Problems of Dostoevsky's Poetics* by R. W. Rotsel (Ann Arbor, MI: Ardis, 1973), and retranslated under the same title by Caryl Emerson (Minneapolis, MN: University of Minnesota Press, 1984; Theory and History of Literature Series, Vol. 8), to which 1984 retranslation page references are keyed in this essay.

1970–1971. "From Notes Made in 1970–1971", a section within the posthumous collection *Estetika slovesnogo tvorchestva* (Moscow, 1979), trans. by Vern W. McGee as *Speech Genres and Other Late Essays*, ed. Caryl Emerson and Michael Holquist (Austin, TX: University of Texas Press, 1986), 132–158.

1975. *Voprosy literatury i estetiki* (Moscow), trans. by Caryl Emerson and Michael Holquist as *The Dialogic Imagination; Four Essays by M. M. Bakhtin*, ed. Michael Holquist (Austin: University of Texas Press, 1981), to which translation page reference is made.

BARGATZKY, Walter.

1978. *Das Universum Lebt: Die Aufsehenerregende Hypothese vom Organischen Aufbau des Weltalls* (Munich: Wilhelm Heyne Verlag).

BARTHES, Roland.

1964. *Éléments de Sémiologie* (Paris: Seuil), trans. by Annette Lavers and Colin Smith as *Elements of Semiology* (New York: Hill and Wang, 1967), to which translation page reference is made in this essay.

1970. *S/Z* (Paris: Seuil), trans. with title unchanged by Richard Miller (New York: Farrar, Straus and Giroux, 1974).

BENTHAM, Jeremy.

1816. *Chrestomathia: Being a Collection of Papers, Explanatory of the Design of an Institution Proposed to be Set on Foot Under the Name of the Chrestomathic Day School, or Chrestomathic School, for the Extension of the New System of Instruction to the Higher Branches of Learning, For the Use of the Middling and Higher Ranks in Life*, in *The Works of Jeremy Bentham*, ed. John Bowring (Edinburgh, 1838–1843; reproduced 1962 by Russell & Russell, Inc., New York), Vol. 8, pp. 1–191, esp. Appendix No. IV, the "Essay on Nomenclature and Classification", 63–128.

BERGER, Arthur Asa.

1982. *Media Analysis Techniques* (London: Sage Publisher).

BERKELEY, George.

1732. *Alciphron, or The Minute Philosopher*, Volume III of *The Works of George Berkeley, Bishop of Cloyne*, ed. T. Jessop (London: Thomas Nelson and Sons, 1950).

BOETHIUS, Anicius Manlius Severinus (chronology based on Cappuyns 1937).

510. *In categorias Aristotelis libri quattuor*, in *PL* 64 (Migne ed.).

511. *In librum Aristotelis de interpretatione Commentaria minor.*

511–513. *In librum Aristotelis de interpretatione Commentaria major.*

BOUISSAC, Paul.

1979. "A Compass for Semiotics", *Ars Semeiotica* 2.2: 205–221.

1981. "Figurative versus Objective Semiotics: an epistemolological crossroads", in *Semiotics 1981*, John N. Deely and Margot D. Lenhart, eds. (New York: Plenum Press), 3–12.

BRUNER, Jerome.
  1984, May 31. Quotation from opening lecture for ISISSS '84 course, "Topics
       in Developmental Pragmatics".
BURKS, Arthur W.
  1958. "Bibliography of the Works of Charles Sanders Peirce", in *The Collected
       Papers of Charles Sanders Peirce*, Volume VIII ed. Arthur W. Burks (Cam-
       bridge, MA: Harvard University Press, 1958), 249–330.
CAJETAN, Thomas de Vio.
  1507. *Commentaria in summam theologicam. Prima pars* (Rome), reprinted in
       Sancti Thomae Aquinatis Doctoris Angelici Opera Omnia, vols. 4 and 5 (Rome:
       Leonine, 1888–1889).
CAPUTO. John.
  1987. *Radical Hermeneutics. Repetition, Deconstruction, and the Hermeneutic Project*
       (Bloomington: Indiana University Press).
CAPPUYNS, M.
  1937. Entry "Boèce" in *Dictionnaire d'Histoire et de Géographie Ecclésiastique*, tome
       neuvième (Paris: Librarie Letouzey), cols. 347–380.
CARLETON, Thomas Compton.
  1649. "De Signo", *Logica*, Disp. 42, in his *Philosophia Universalis* (Antwerp).
       Commentary in Doyle 1988, q.v.
CHENU, Joseph, ed.
  1984. *Peirce. Textes Anticarlésiens*, présentation et traduction de Joseph Chenu
       (Paris: Aubier, 1984).
CHOMSKY, Noam.
  1968. *Language and Mind* (New York: Harcourt, Brace, & World).
CLARKE, David S.
  1987. *Principles of Semiotic* (London: Routledge & Kegan Paul).
CON DAVIS, Robert.
  1985. "The Case for a Post-Structuralist Mimesis: John Barth and Imitation",
       in *The American Journal of Semiotics* 3.3, 49–72.
CONIMBRICENSES.
  1607. "De Signis", being Chapter 1 of their commentary on Aristotle's *De
       Interpretatione*, in *Commentarii Collegii Conimbricensis et Societatis Jesu. In
       Universam Dialecticam Aristotelis Stagiritae. Secunda Pars* (Lyons: Sumpti-
       bus Horatii Cardon).
CRAIK, K. J. W.
  1967. *The Nature of Explanation* (Cambridge: Cambridge University Press).
CULLER, Jonathan.
  1977. *Ferdinand de Saussure* (New York: Penguin).
  1981. *The Pursuit of Signs. Semiotics, Literature, Deconstruction* (Ithaca, NY: Cor-
       nell University Press).
  1982. *On Deconstruction. Theory and Criticism after Structuralism* (Ithaca, NY:
       Cornell University Press).
CUNNINGHAM, Donald C.
  1988. "Abduction and Affordance: J. J. Gibson and Theories of Semiosis", in
       Semiotics 1988, ed. Terry Prewitt, John Deely, and Karen Haworth
       (Lanham, MD: University Press of America, 1989), 27–33.
DANOW, David.
  1987. "Text and Subtext", in *Semiotics 1987*, ed. John Deely (Lanham, MD: Uni-
       versity Press of America, 1988).

DE GEORGE, Richard T., ed.
1981.   *Semiotic Themes* (=University of Kansas Humanistic Studies 53; Lawrence: University of Kansas Publications).
DEELY, John.
1969.   "The Philosophical Dimensions of the Origin of Species," *The Thomist* XXXIII (January and April), Part I, 75–149, Part II, 251–342.
1971.   "Animal Intelligence and Concept-Formation," *The Thomist* XXXV. 1 (January), 43–93.
1975.   "Reference to the Nonexistent", *The Thomist* XXXIX.2 (April), 253–308.
1978.   "Semiotic and the Controversy over Mental Events", ACPA *Proceedings* LII, 16–27.
1978a. "What's in a Name?", *Semiotica* 22.1/2, 151–181 (essay review of original 1976 publication of Sebeok 1985).
1981.   "Cognition from a Semiotic Point of View", in *Semiotics 1981*, ed. John N. Deely and Margot D. Lenhart (New York: Plenum, 1983), 21–28.
1982.   *Introducing Semiotic: Its History and Doctrine* (Bloomington: Indiana University Press).
1982a. "On the Notion of Phytosemiotics", in *Semiotics 1982*, ed. John Deely and Jonathan Evans (Lanham, MD: University Press of America, 1987), 541–554; reprinted with minor revision in Deely, Williams, and Kruse 1986: 96–103.
1982b. "On the Notion 'Doctrine of Signs'", Appendix I in Deely 1982: 127–130.
1984.   "Semiotic as Framework and Direction", in Deely, Kruse, and Williams, eds., 1986: 264–271.
1985.   "Editorial Afterword" to *Tractatus de Signis: The Semiotic of John Poinsot* (Berkeley: University of California Press), 391–514.
1985a. *Logic as a Liberal Art* (Victoria University: Toronto Semiotic Circle Monograph, Summer 1985). Extensive discussion of Umwelt, Innenwelt, and related notions.
1985b. "Semiotic and the Liberal Arts", *The New Scholasticism* LIX.3 (Summer), 296–322.
1986.   "A Context for Narrative Universals, or: Semiology as a Pars Semeiotica", in *The American Journal of Semiotics* 4.3/4, 53–68.
1986a. "John Locke's Place in the History of Semiotic Inquiry", in *Semiotics 1986*, ed. Jonathan Evans and John Deely (Lanham, MD: University Press of America, 1987), 406–418.
1986b. "Doctrine", terminological entry for the *Encyclopedic Dictionary of Semiotics* ed. Thomas A. Sebeok et al. (Berlin: Mouton), Tome I, p. 214.
1986c. "The Coalescence of Semiotic Consciousness", in Deely, Williams, and Kruse 1986: 5–34.
1986d. "Semiotic in the Thought of Jacques Maritain", *Recherche Sémiotique/ Semiotic Inquiry* 6.2, 1–30.
1986e. "Idolum. Archeology and Ontology of the Iconic Sign", in *Iconicity: Essays on the Nature of Culture*, Festschrift volume in honor of Thomas A. Sebeok, edited by Paul Bouissac, Michael Herzfeld, and Roland Posner (Tubingen: Stauffenburg Verlag), 29–49.
1987.   "On the Problem of Interpreting the Term 'First' in the Expression 'First Philosophy'", in *Semiotics 1987*, ed. J. Deely (Lanham, MD: University Press of America), 3–14.
1988.   "The Semiotic of John Poinsot: Yesterday and Tomorrow", major discus-

sion of reviews of and theoretical issues in the 1631–1632 work of Poinsot (1985 scholarly edition, above), *Semiotica* 69.1/2 (April), 31–127.

1988a. "Semiotics and First Philosophy", in *Hermeneutics and the Tradition*, ACPA Proceedings Vol. LXII, ed. Daniel O. Dahlstrom (Washington, DC), 136–146.

1989. "A Global Enterprise", Preface to Thomas A. Sebeok, *The Sign & Its Masters* (= Sources in Semiotics VIII; Lanham, MD: University Press of America, 1989), vii-xiv.

DEELY, John N., and Margot D. LENHART, eds.

1981. *Semiotics 1981* (Proceedings of the Sixth Annual Meeting of the Semiotic Society of America; New York: Plenum Press).

DEELY, John N., Brooke WILLIAMS, and Felicia E. KRUSE, editors.

1986. *Frontiers in Semiotics* (Bloomington: Indiana University Press). Preface titled "Pars Pro Toto", pp. viii-xvii.

DESCARTES, René.

1637. *Discourse on the Method of Rightly Conducting the Reason and Seeking for Truth in the Sciences*, trans. Elizabeth S. Haldane and G. R. T. Gross in *The Philosophical Works of Descartes* (corrected reprint edition; New York: Dover, 1955, I: 79–130.

1641. *Meditations on First Philosophy*, trans. Elizabeth S. Haldane and G. R. T. Gross in *The Philosophical Works of Descartes* (corrected reprint edition; New York: Dover, 1955), I, 131–199.

DOYLE, John P.

1984. "The Conimbricenses on the Relations Involved in Signs", in *Semiotics 1984*, ed. John Deely (Lanham, MD: University Press of America), 567–576.

1984a. "Prolegomena to a Study of Extrinsic Denomination in the Work of Francis Suarez, S.J.", *Vivarium* 22.2, 121–160.

1988. "Thomas Compton Carleton, S.J.: On Words Signifying More Than Their Speakers or Makers Intend", in *The Modern Schoolman* LXVI (November), 1–28.

ECO, Umberto.

1973. *O Signo*, trans. into Portuguese by Maria de Fatima Marinho (3a ed.; Lisbon: Editorial Presença) of *Segno* (Milan: Istituto Editoriale Internazionale).

1976. *A Theory of Semiotics* (Bloomington: Indiana University Press).

1977. "The Code: Metaphor or Interdisciplinary Category?", in *Yale Italian Studies* 1.1 (Winter), 24–52.

1979. "Proposals for a History of Semiotics", in *Semiotics Unfolding*, ed. Tasso Borbé (Berlin: Mouton), 75–89.

1980. "The Sign Revisited", in *Philosophy and Social Criticism* 7.3/4, 263–297.

1982. "On Symbols", *Recherche Sémiotique/Semiotic Inquiry* 2.1 (March 1982), 15–44, reprinted with corrections as Ch. 4 of Eco 1984. The 1982 and 1984 texts were critically compared and further improved in the reprint in Deely, Williams, and Kruse 1986: 153–180, q.v.

1984. *Semiotics and the Philosophy of Language* (Bloomington: Indiana University Press). Includes some treatment of Stoic and early Latin ideas important for semiotics.

ECO, Umberto, and John DEELY.

1983. May 30-June 24. "Historiographical Foundations of Semiotics", course taught at ISISSS '83 (Indiana University, Bloomington campus).

ECO, Umberto, Roberto LAMBERTINI, Costantino MARMO, and Andrea TABARRONI.

1986. "Latratus Canis or: The Dog's Barking", in Deely, Williams, and Kruse 1986: 63–73; see the editorial note on the background of this text, ibid. p. xix.

ESCHBACH, Achim, and Jurgen TRABANT, eds.

1983. *History of Semiotics* (Amsterdam: John Benjamins), esp. "2.1. Ancient and Medieval Semiotics", 39–144.

ESSLIN, Martin.

1987. *The Field of Drama* (London: Methuen).

FISCH, Max H.

1986. Review by Max H. Fisch of Poinsot 1632a in *New Vico Studies*, ed. Giorgio Tagliacozzo and Donald Phillip Verene (New York: Humanities Press International, Inc., for The Institute for Vico Studies), Volume IV, pp. 178–182.

FISCH, Max H., Kenneth Laine KETNER, and Christian J. W. KLOESEL.

1979. "The New Tools of Peirce Scholarship, with Particular Reference to Semiotic", in *Peirce Studies* 1 (Lubbock, TX: Institute for Studies in Pragmaticism), 1–17.

FONSECA, Petrus.

1564. *Instituições Dialecticas (Institutionum Dialecticarum Libri Octo)*, ed. Joaquim Ferreira Gomes (Coimbra: Instituto de Estudos Filosóficos da Universidade de Coimbra, 1964), 2 volumes.

von FRISCH, Karl.

1950. *Bees, Their Vision, Chemical Senses, and Language* (Ithaca: Cornell University Press).

FURTON, Edward J.

1987. Review of Poinsot 1632a/Deely 1985 in *Summaries and Comments* (June).

GIBSON, J.

1979. *The Ecological Approach to Visual Perception* (Bloomington: Indiana University Press).

GOULD, Stephen J., and Elisabeth S. VRBA.

1982. "Exaptation—A Missing Term in the Science of Form", *Paleobiology* 8.1 (Winter), 4–15.

HALL, Edward T.

1976. *Beyond Culture* (New York: Doubleday & Company).

HARDWICK, Charles, Editor.

1977. *Semiotics and Significs. The Correspondence between Charles S. Peirce and Victoria Lady Welby* (Bloomington: Indiana University Press, 1977).

HAWKES, Terence.

1977. *Structuralism and Semiotics* (Berkeley: University of California Press).

HAWKING, Stephen A.

1988. *A Brief History of Time, from the Big Bang to Black Holes* (New York: Bantam Books).

HEIDEGGER, Martin.

1927. *Sein und Zeit* (10th ed.; Tübingen: Niemeyer, 1963).

HENDERSON, Lawrence J.

1913. *The Fitness of the Environment* (Boston: Beacon Press).

HENRY, D. P.

1987. "The Way to Awareness", review of Poinsot 1632a/Deely 1985 in *The Times*

Literary Supplement no. 4,413 (October 30-November 5, 1987), p. 1201.

HJELSMSLEV, Louis.
1961. *Prolegomena to a Theory of Language*, being the second, revised translation by Francis J. Whitfield of *Omkring sprogteoriens grundlæggelse* (Copenhagen: Ejnar Munksgaard, 1943), incorporating "several minor corrections and changes that have suggested themselves in the course of discussions between the author and the translator" (Hjelmslev and Whitfield, page v of this volume).

HUME, David.
1748. *An Enquiry concerning Human Understanding*, complete and unabridged text in *The English Philosophers from Bacon to Mill*, ed. E. A. Burtt (New York: The Modern Library, 1939), 585–689.

JAKOBSON, Roman.
1979. "Coup d'oeil sur le devéloppement de la sémiotique", in *Panorama Sémiotique/A Semiotic Landscape*, ed. Seymour Chatman, Umberto Eco, and Jean-Marie Klinkenberg (Proceedings of the International Association for Semiotic Studies, Milan, June 1974; The Hague: Mouton), 3–18.

JAMESON, Fredric.
1972. *The Prison House of Language: A Critical Account of Structuralism and Russian Formalism* (Princeton: Princeton University Press).

JOHANSEN, Jørgen Dines.
1982. "Sign Concept, Meaning, and the Study of Literature", in *Semiotics 1982*, ed. John Deely and Jonathan Evans (Lanham, MD: University Press of America, 1987), 473–482.
1985. "Prolegomena to a Semiotic Theory of Text Interpretation", *Semiotica* 57.3/4, 225–288.

JOYCE, James.
1939. *Finnegans Wake* (London: Faber & Faber).

KANT, Immanuel.
1781, 1787. *Kritik der reinen Vernunft* (Riga), English trans. by Norman Kemp Smith, *Kant's Critique of Pure Reason* (New York: St. Martin's Press, 1963).

KENT, Beverly.
1987. *Charles S. Peirce: Logic and the Classification of the Sciences* (Montreal: McGill-Queens University Press).

KESSEL, Edward L.
1955. "The Mating Activities of Balloon Flies", *Systematic Zoology* 4, 96–104.

KING, Terrance.
1987. "Text and Object: Distinguishing Them as Interpretations", in *Semiotics 1987* (Lanham, MD: University Press of America, 1988), 99–106.

KOELB, Clayton, and Virgil LOKKE, Editors.
1988. *The Current in Criticism. Essays on the Present and Future of Literary Theory* (West Lafayette, IN: Purdue University Press).

KRAMPEN, Martin.
1981. "Phytosemiotics", *Semiotica* 36.3/4, 187–209; substantially reprinted in Deely, Williams, and Kruse 1986: 83–95.

KRUSE. Felicia E.
1986. "Saving the Sign", in *Semiotics 1986*, ed. John Deely and Jonathan Evans (Lanham, MD: University Press of America, 1987), 277–284.

LACHELIER, Jules.
1933. *Oeuvres de Jules Lachelier*, Tome I (Paris: Alcan).

LINGUISTIC SOCIETY OF PARIS, STATUTES ("Statuts" de la Société de Linguistique de Paris).
1868.   *Memoires de la Société de Linguistique de Paris* (Paris: Librairie A. Franck),
Vol. I, p. 3.
LOCKE, John.
1690.   *An Essay Concerning Humane Understanding* (London: Thomas Bassett).
The original text of the concluding chapter introducing the term "semiotic" is reproduced in full from this original edition in Deely, Williams,
and Kruse 1986: 2–4.
LOVELOCK, J. E.
1972.   "Gaia as Seen through the Atmosphere", *Atmosphere and Environment* 6,
579–580.
1979.   *Gaia. A New Look at Life on Earth* (Oxford, England: Oxford University
Press).
1988.   *The Ages of Gaia: A Biography of Our Living Earth* (New York: W. W. Norton).
MACKINNON, D. L., Translator.
1926.   *Theoretical Biology*, being an attempted translation of von Uexküll 1920
(New York: Harcourt Brace & Co.). Hopefully, another attempt will be
made, this time within the perspective of semiotic.
MARGULIS, Lynn, and Dorian SAGAN.
1986.   *Microcosmos: Four Billion Years of Evolution From Our Microbial Ancestors*
(New York: Summit).
1986a.   *Origins of Sex: Three Billion Years of Genetic Recombination* (New Haven: Yale
University Press).
MARITAIN, Jacques.
1937–1938.   "Sign and Symbol", trans. Mary Morris in *Journal of the Warburg Institute* I, 1–11. The French text from which Morris worked in marking this
translation seems never to have been published except as incorporated
in a much expanded version of this essay which appeared in French the
following year as "Signe et Symbole" in the *Revue Thomiste* XLIV (avril),
299–330. A nearly complete tracing of Maritain's reflections as begun in
this early essay can be found in Deely 1986d, q.v.
1957.   "Language and the Theory of Sign", originally published as Chapter V
of the anthology *Language: An Enquiry into Its Meaning and Function* edited
by Ruth Nanda Anshen (New York: Harper & Bros.), 86–101, is reprinted
with the addition of a full technical apparatus explicitly connecting the
essay to Maritain's work on semiotic begun in 1937 and to the text of
Poinsot 1632 on which Maritain centrally drew, in Deely et al. 1986:
51–62, to which reprint page references are keyed.
1964.   *Notebooks*, Chapter 3 (translated by Joseph W. Evans; New York: Albany,
1984), 81–99.
MATES, Benson.
1953.   *Stoic Logic* (Berkeley: University of California Press; 2nd printing, with
a new Preface, 1961).
MAYR, Ernst.
1974.   "Teleological and Teleonomic: A New Analysis", in *Methodological and Historical Essays in the Natural and Social Sciences*, 4, ed. Robert S. Cohen and
Marx W. Wartofsky (Dordrecht, Holland: D. Reidel Publishing Co.),
91–117.
1983.   Adaptation of 1974 entry with unchanged title as Chapter 25 of *Evolution*

and the Diversity of Life. Selected Essays (Cambridge, MA: The Belknap Press of Harvard University Press), 383–404.

MCKEON, Richard.
  1941. *The Basic Works of Aristotle* (New York: Random House).
MEAD, Margaret.
  1964. "Vicissitudes of the Study of the Total Communication Process", in *Approaches to Semiotics. Cultural Anthropology. Education. Linguistics. Psychiatry. Psychology (Transactions of the Indiana University Conference on Paralinguistics and Kinesics)*, ed. Thomas A. Sebeok, Alfred S. Hayes, and Mary Catherine Bateson (The Hague: Mouton), 277–287.
MERRELL, Floyd.
  1987. "Of Position Papers, Paradigms, and Paradoxes", *Semiotica* 65.3/4, 191–223.
  1988. "An Uncertain Semiotic", in *The Current in Criticism. Essays on the Present and Future of Literary Theory*, ed. Clayton Koelb and Virgil Lokke (West Lafayette, IN: Purdue University Press), 243–264.
MILLER, Eugene F.
  1979. "Hume's Reduction of Cause to Sign", *The New Scholasticism* LIII.1, 42–75.
MONOD, Jacques.
  1970. *Le Hasard et la Necessité: essai sur la philosophie naturelle de la biologie moderne* (Paris: Seuil).
MORGAN, Thaïs.
  1985. "Is There an Intertext in This Text: Literary and Interdisciplinary Approaches to Intertextuality", *The American Journal of Semiotics* 3.4, 1–40.
MORRIS, Charles.
  1946. *Signs, Language and Behavior* (Englewood Cliffs, NJ: Prentice-Hall); reprinted complete in Charles Morris, *Writings on the General Theory of Signs*, ed. Thomas A. Sebeok (= Approaches to Semiotics 16; The Hague: Mouton, 1971), 73–397.
MOUNIN, Georges.
  1970. *Introduction à la sémiologie* (Paris: Minuit).
OCKHAM, William of.
  i. 1317–1328. *Summa Logicae*, ed. Philotheus Boehner (New York: St. Bonaventure, 1951–1954).
PARRET, Herman.
  1984. "Peirce and Hjelmslev: The Two Semiotics", *Language Sciences* 6.2, 217–227.
PEIRCE, Charles Sanders.
  Note: The designation CP abbreviates *The Collected Papers of Charles Sanders Peirce*, Vols. I-VI ed. Charles Hartshorne and Paul Weiss (Cambridge, MA: Harvard University Press, 1931–1935), Vols. VII-VIII ed. Arthur W. Burks (same publisher, 1958). The abbreviation followed by volume and paragraph numbers with a period between follows the standard CP reference form.
  The designation NEM abbreviates *The New Elements of Mathematics*, ed. Carolyn Eisele (The Hague: Mouton, 1976), 4 volumes bound as 5.
  The designation W followed by volume and page numbers with a period in between abbreviates the ongoing *Writings of Charles S. Peirce: A Chronological Edition*, initiated as the Peirce Edition Project at Indiana University-Purdue University/Indianapolis by Edward C. Moore under

the general editorship of Max H. Fisch, now under the direction of Christian Kloesel (Bloomington: Indiana University Press, 3 vols.—1982, 1984, 1986—of a projected 20 published so far).

Unpublished mss. are cited by number, using the pagination made by the Institute for Studies in Pragmaticism at Texas Tech in Lubbock.

Chronology and identification of the Peirce materials is based on Burks 1958, Fisch et al. 1979, Hardwick 1977, and Robin 1967, 1971, as indicated at specific points.

1867. "On a New List of Categories", CP 1.545–567 (Burks p. 261); W 2.49–59.

1867a. "Upon Logical Comprehension and Extension", *Proceedings of the American Academy of Arts and Sciences*, 7 (November 13, 1867), 416–432, with additions and corrections c.1870 and 1893; CP 2.391–426, 427–430 (Burks 261, 280).

1868. "Some Consequences of Four Incapacities", in CP 5.310–317; W 2.241.

c.1890. "A Guess at the Riddle", CP 1.354–416 (Burks p. 276).

1892. "The Law of Mind", *The Monist* (2 July), 533–559; reprinted in CP 6.102–163.

1892a. "Man's Glassy Essence", *The Monist* (3 October), 1–22; reprinted in CP 6.238–271.

c.1896. "The Logic of Mathematics; An Attempt To Develop My Categories from Within", CP 1.417–520 (Burks p. 281).

1897. "The Logic of Relatives", CP 3.456–552 (Burks p. 287).

c.1899. A fragment of biographical comments: CP 1.3–7 (Burks p. 287).

c.1902. Ms. 599, "Reason's Rules" (Robin p. 74), partially included in CP 5.538–545.

c.1902a. "Minute Logic", draft for a book complete consecutively only to Chapter 4. Published in CP in extracts scattered over six of the eight volumes, including 1.203–283, 1.575–584; 2.1–202, 2.757n1; 4.227–323; 6.349–352; 7.279, 7.374n10, 7.362–387 except 381n19. (For fuller detail, see Burks 293–294).

1903. Lowell Lectures, "Some Topics of Logic Bearing on Questions Now Vexed", esp.: lect. IIIA, "Lessons from the History of Philosophy", CP 1.15–26; draft 3 of lect. 3 entitled "Degenerate Cases", in CP 1.521–544; lect. 8, "How to Theorize", CP 5.590–604 (Burks p. 295); and the section published in CP 4.510–529 under the title "The Gamma Part of Existential Graphs".

1903a. "Lectures on Pragmatism", esp. lect. V, "The Three Kinds of Goodness", CP 5.120–150 (Burks pp. 204–205).

1904. "On Signs and the Categories", from a letter to Lady Welby dated 12 October, in CP 8.327–341 (Burks p. 321).

1905. Review of Wilhelm Wundt's *Principles of Physiological Psychology*, Vol. 1, 81 (July 20), pp. 56–57, also in *New York Evening Post* (21 July) 4, 1–3; in CP 8.96–204 (Burks p. 316 n. 19).

1905–1906. Ms. 283, partially published under the title "The Basis of Pragmaticism" in CP 1.573–574 (= ms. pp. 37–45), 5.549–554 (= ms. pp. 45–59), and 5.448n. (= ms. pp. 135–148) (Burks p. 328 and 298).

1906, March 9. 52-page draft letter to Lady Welby (under Robin L463, p. 200), ms. pp. 24–30 excerpted in Hardwick 1977: 195–201, to which published excerpt page reference is made in this work.

c.1907. "Pragmatism", MS 318 in the Robin *Annotated Catalogue* (1967). (A small segment of this ms. appears under the title "From Pragmatism" in NEM III.1: 481–494).

c. 1907a. Excerpt from "Pragmatism (Editor [3])", published under the title "A Survey of Pragmaticism" in CP 5.464–496. (Burks p. 299).

1908. "A Neglected Argument for the Reality of God", CP 6.452–485 (Burks p. 300).

1908a. Letter to Lady Welby begun December 14 (in Hardwick 1977: 63–73) and continued December 23 (ibid.: 73–86); the "sop to Cerberus passage" occurs in the latter part.

1908b. Draft of a letter dated December 24, 25, 28 "On the Classification of Signs", CP 8.342–379 except 368n23 are from it (Burks p. 321 par. 20.b).

1909. From a letter dated March 14, printed under the heading "Signs" in CP 8.314 (Burks p. 320 par. 14.b).

c. 1909. "Some Amazing Mazes, Fourth Curiosity", CP 6.318–348.

PENCAK, William.
1986. "Carl Becker and the Semiotics of History", in Semiotics 1986, ed. John Deely and Jonathan Evans (Lanham, MD: University Press of America, 1987), 443–451.

PERCIVAL, W. Keith.
1981. "Ferdinand de Saussure and the History of Semiotics", in De George 1981, q.v.

PERRON, Paul.
1983. "Preface" to Paris School Semiotics: Texts and Documents. I. Theory (Toronto Semiotic Circle Monograph).

PIGNATARI, Decio.
1971. Informação. Linguagem. Communicação (5th ed.: São Paulo: Perspectiva).

PITTENDRIGH, Colin S.
1958. "Adaptation, Natural Selection, and Evolution", Chapter 18 of Behavior and Evolution, ed. Anne Roe and George Gaylord Simpson (New Haven: Yale University Press), 390–416.

PLATO.
c. 385BC. Cratylus, trans. Benjamin Jowett in The Collected Dialogues of Plato Including the Letters, ed. Edith Hamilton and Huntington Cairns (Bollingen Series LXXI; New York: Pantheon Books, 1961), 421–474.

POINSOT, John.
Note: A complete table of all the editions, complete and partial, and in whatever language, of Poinsot's systematic works in philosophy and theology is provided in Deely 1985: 396–397. The principal modern editions referred to in this work are abbreviated as follows:

R followed by a volume number (I, II, or III) and pages, with column (a or b) and line indications as needed = the Cursus Philosophicus Thomisticus, ed. by B. Reiser in 3 volumes (Turin: Marietti, 1930, 1933, 1937).

S followed by a volume number (I-IV) and page numbers = the five volumes of the incomplete critical edition of the Cursus Theologicus ed. at Solesmes (Paris: Desclée, 1931, 1934, 1937, 1946; Matiscone: Protat Frères, 1953).

V followed by a volume number (I-IX) = the complete edition ed. by Ludovicus Vivès published in Paris between 1883 and 1886.

1631. Artis Logicae Prima Pars (Alcalá, Spain). The opening pages 1–11a14 of this work and the "Quaestio Disputanda I. De Termino. Art. 6. Utrum

Voces Significant per prius Conceptus an Res" pages 104b31–108a33, relevant to the discussion of signs in the *Secunda Pars* of 1632 (entry following), have been incorporated in the 1632a entry (second entry following, q.v., pp. 4–30 and 342–351 "Appendix A. On the Signification of Language", respectively), for the independent edition of that discussion published by the University of California Press. From R I: 1–247.

1632. *Artis Logicae Secunda Pars* (Alcalá, Spain). From R I: 249–839.

1632a. *Tractatus de Signis*, subtitled *The Semiotic of John Poinsot*, extracted from the *Artis Logicae Prima et Secunda Pars* of 1631–1632 (above two entries) and arranged in bilingual format by John Deely in consultation with Ralph A. Powell (First Edition; Berkeley: University of California Press, 1985), as explained in Deely 1985, q.v. Pages in this volume are set up in matching columns of English and Latin, with intercolumnar numbers every fifth line. (Thus, references to the volume are by page number, followed by a slash and the appropriate line number of the specific section of text referred to—e.g., 287/3–26.)

1633. *Naturalis Philosophiae Prima Pars* (Madrid, Spain). In R II: 1–529.

1634. *Naturalis Philosophiae Tertia Pars* (Alcalá, Spain); in Reiser vol. II: 533–888.

1635. *Naturalis Philosophiae Quarta Pars* (Alcalá, Spain); in Reiser vol. III: 1–425.

1637. *Tomus Primus Cursus Theologici* (Alcalá, Spain). V I & II; S I complete & II through p. 529.

POWELL, Ralph A.

1983. *Freely Chosen Reality* (Lanham, MD: University Press of America).

1986. "From Semiotic of Scientific Mechanism to Semiotic of Teleology in Nature", in *Semiotics 1986*, ed. John Deely and Jonathan Evans (Lanham, MD: University Press of America), 296–305.

1988. "Degenerate Secondness in Peirce's Belief in God", in *ACPA Proceedings* LXII.

1988a. "Epistemology's Minimal Cause as Basis of Science", *Semiotics 1988*, ed. Terry Prewitt, John Deely, and Karen Haworth (13th Annual Proceedings of the Semiotic Society of America; Lanham, MD: University Press of America), 180–188.

RANSDELL, Joseph.

1977. "Some Leading Ideas of Peirce's Semiotic", *Semiotica* 19, 157–178.

RAUCH, Irmengard.

1983. "'Symbols Grow': Creation, Compulsion, Change", SSA Presidential Address (Snowbird, Utah), subsequently published in *The American Journal of Semiotics* 3.1 (1984), 2–23.

REISER, B., ed.

1930–1937. The 1631–1635 *Cursus Philosophicus* of John Poinsot, arranged in three volumes (Turin: Marietti; vol. I, 1930; vol. 2, 1933; vol. 3, 1937), as explained in detail under entry for Poinsot above.

RICOEUR, Paul.

1981. *Hermeneutics & the Human Sciences*, ed. and trans. John B. Thompson (Cambridge: Cambridge University Press).

ROBIN, Richard S.

1967. *Annotated Catalogue of the Papers of Charles S. Peirce* (Worcester, MA: The University of Massachusetts Press).

1971. "The Peirce Papers: A Supplementary Catalogue", *Transactions of the Charles S. Peirce Society* VII.1 (Winter), 37–57.

ROMEO, Luigi.
  1976.   "Heraclitus and the Foundations of Semiotics", *Versus* 15 (dicembre), 73–90.
  1977.   "The Derivation of 'Semiotics' through the History of the Discipline", in *Semiosis* 6 (ed. M. Bense, G. Deledalle, and E. Walther), Heft 2, 37–49.
  1979.   "Pedro da Fonseca in Renaissance Semiotics: A Segmental History of Footnotes", *Ars Semeiotica* 3, 3–32.
RUSSELL, Anthony F.
  1982.   "The Semiosis Linking Human World and Physical Reality", in *Semiotics 1982* (Lanham, MD: University Press of America, 1987), 591–600.
  1984.   *Logic, Philosophy, and History* (=Sources in Semiotics 1; Lanham, MD: University Press of America).
SAGAN, Dorion, and Lynn MARGULIS.
  1987.   "Bacterial Bedfellows", *Natural History* 96.3, 26–33.
de SAUSSURE, Ferdinand.
  i. 1906–1911.   Lectures delivered at the University of Geneva and published from auditors' notes by Charles Bally and Albert Sechehaye with the collaboration of Albert Riedlinger under the title *Cours de Linguistique Generale* in 1916; critical edition prepared by Tullio de Mauro (Paris: Payot, 1972). English trans. with annotations by Roy Harris, *Course in General Linguistics* (London: Duckworth, 1983). This English edition includes the page numbers of the French original in square brackets in the margins. References in the present work are to this bracketed pagination.
SAVAN, David.
  1986.   "Skeptics", in the *Encyclopedic Dictionary of Semiotics* ed. Thomas A. Sebeok et al. (Berlin: Mouton), 954–957.
  1986a.   "Stoicism", in the *Encyclopedic Dictionary of Semiotics* ed. Thomas A. Sebeok et al. (Berlin: Mouton), 976–980.
SCHILLER, Claire H.
  1957.   "Note by the Translator" to *Instinctive Behavior. The Development of a Modern Concept* (New York: International Universities Press, 1957), with particular reference to von Uexküll 1934, q.v.
SCHOLES, Robert.
  1982.   *Semiotics and Interpretation* (New Haven, CT: Yale University Press).
SCOTUS, Joannes Duns.
  c. 1302–1303.   *Ordinatio, Liber Primus*, Volume III of the *Opera Omnia*, ed. P. Carolus Balic (Rome: Typis Polyglottis Vaticanis, 1954).
SEBEOK, Thomas Albert.
  1963.   "Review of Communication among Social Bees; Porpoises and Sonar; Man and Dolphin", in *Language* 39.3, 448–466, partially reprinted in Deely et al. 1986: 74–75, to which excerpt page reference is made in this volume.
  1968.   "Is a Comparative Semiotics Possible?", in *Échanges et Communications: Mélanges offerts à Claude Lévi-Strauss à l'occasion de son 60ème anniversaire*, ed. Jean Pouillon and Pierre Maranda (The Hague: Mouton), 614–627; reprinted in Sebeok 1985: 59–69, to which page reference is made.
  1971   (original draft). "'Semiotics' and Its Congeners", reprinted in Sebeok 1976a: 47–58, to which reprint page reference is made here.
  1974.   "Semiotics: A Survey of the State of the Art", in *Linguistics and Adjacent Arts and Sciences*, Vol. 12 of the *Current Trends in Linguistics* series, ed. T.

A. Sebeok (The Hague: Mouton), 211–264; reprinted in Sebeok 1985: 1–45, to which page reference is made.

1974a. "La dynamique des signes", in *L'Unité de l'homme: Invariants biologiques et universaux culturels*, ed. Edgar Morin and Massimo Piattelli-Palmiarini (Paris: Éditions de Seuil), 61–77; reprinted in Sebeok 1985: 95–110, to which page reference is made.

1975. "The Semiotic Web: A Chronicle of Prejudices", *Bulletin of Literary Semiotics* 2, 1–63, as reprinted with essential corrections and additions in Sebeok 1985: 149–188.

1976. "Final Report: Narrative" for the National Endowment for the Humanities on the Pilot Program in Semiotics in the Humanities at Indiana University's Bloomington campus, 1 August 1975–31 July 1976 (report dated June 1, 1976, distributed by the Research Center for Language and Semiotic Studies at IU Bloomington, 14 pages; subsequently published as "Appendix III. Teaching Semiotics: Report on a Pilot Program", in Sebeok 1989: 272–279).

1976a. "Foreword" (pp. ix-xiii) to original publication of Sebeok 1985 following.

1977. "Ecumenicalism in Semiotics", in *A Perfusion of Signs*, ed. Thomas A. Sebeok (Bloomington: Indiana University Press), 180–206.

1977a. "The Semiotic Self", discussion paper presented at the Werner-Reimers-Stiftung, in Germany, and subsequently included as Appendix I in Sebeok 1989: 263–267.

1979. "Neglected Figures in the History of Semiotic Inquiry: Jakob von Uexküll", Chapter 10 of Sebeok 1989: 187–207.

1981. "Karl Bühler: A Neglected Figure in the History of Semiotic Inquiry", in *The Play of Musement*, Chapter 5 (Bloomington: Indiana University Press), 91–108.

1982. "Foreword" to *Introducing Semiotic* (Deely 1982, above).

1984. June 3. "The Evolution of Communication and the Origin of Language", lecture in the June 1–3 ISISSS '84 Colloquium on "Phylogeny and Ontogeny of Communication Systems". Published under the title "Communication, Language, and Speech. Evolutionary Considerations", in Sebeok 1986a: 10–16.

1984a. "Vital Signs", Presidential Address delivered October 12 to the ninth Annual Meeting of the Semiotic Society of America, Bloomington, Indiana, October 11–14; subsequently printed in *The American Journal of Semiotics* 3.3, 1–27, and reprinted in Sebeok 1986a: 59–79.

1984b. "Signs of Life", *International Semiotic Spectrum* 2 (June), 1–2.

1984c. "Symptom", Chapter 10 of *New Directions in Linguistics and Semiotics*, ed. James E. Copeland (Houston: Rice University Studies), 212–230.

1985. *Contributions to the Doctrine of Signs* (= Sources in Semiotics IV; reprint of 1976 original with an extended Preface by Brooke Williams, "Challenging Signs at the Crossroads" [Williams 1985a], evaluating the book in light of major reviews; Lanham, MD: University Press of America).

1986. "The Doctrine of Signs", in Deely, Williams, and Kruse 1986: 35–42.

1986a. *I Think I Am A Verb. More Contributions to the Doctrine of Signs* (New York: Plenum Press).

1987. "Language: How Primary a Modeling System?", in *Semiotics 1987*, ed. John Deely (Lanham, MD: University Press of America, 1988), 15–27.

1988. "The Notion 'Semiotic Self' Revisited", in *Semiotics 1988*, ed. Terry Prewitt, John Deely, and Karen Haworth (Lanham, MD: University Press of America, 1989), 189–195.

1989. *The Sign & Its Masters* (= Sources in Semiotics VIII; Lanham, MD: University Press of America. Corrected reprint, with a new Author's Preface and an added Editor's Preface [Deely 1989], of the University of Texas Press 1979 original imprint).

1989a. "The Semiotic Self Revisited", in *Sign, Self, and Society*, ed. Benjamin Lee and Greg Urban (Berlin: Mouton de Gruyter).

1989b? "Semiotics in the United States", introduction to *American Signatures* (Norman: University of Oklahoma Press). Page references are to the manuscript version.

SEXTUS EMPIRICUS (approx. 150–225AD).

c.200fl. *Sextus Empiricus*, Loeb Classical Library Edition of his Greek text with facing English trans. by R. G. Bury (London: Heinemann, 1917–1955), in 4 volumes.

SHANK, Gary D.

1984. June 12. ISISSS '84 Workshop Series on "Theory and Method for Semiotic Research in Psychology", Workshop #2, "Semiosis as a Psychologically Embodied Phenomenon".

SHORT, T. L.

1988. "Why We Prefer Peirce to Saussure", in *Semiotics 1988*, ed. Terry Prewitt, John Deely, and Karen Haworth (Lanham, MD: University Press of America, 1989), 124–130.

SIMPSON, George Gaylord, Colin S. PITTENDRIGH, and Lewis H. TIFFANY.

1957. *Life. An Introduction to Biology* (New York: Harcourt, Brace and Co.).

SOLESMES, ed.

1932–1953. The 1637–1644 *Cursus Theologicus* of John Poinsot, original tomes 1–4 in 5 volumes (Paris: Desclée, vol. I, 1931; vol. 2, 1934; vol. 3, 1937; vol. 4, 1946; Matiscone: Protat Frères, vol. 5, 1946, 1953 with added Preface); incomplete critical edition; see Poinsot entry above.

SOTO, Dominic.

1529, 1554. *Summulae* (1st ed., Burgos; 3rd rev. ed., Salamanca; Facsimile of 3rd ed., Hildesheim, NY: Georg Olms Verlag).

SUAREZ, Francis.

1597. *Disputationes Metaphysicae* (Salamanca), vols. 25–26 of the *Opera Omnia*, new ed. by Carolus Berton (Paris: Vivès, 1861).

TODOROV, Tzvetan.

1981. *Mikhail Bakhtine: Le Principe Dialogique Suivi de Écrits da Cercle de Bakhtine*, trans. from the French by Wlad Godzich as *Mikhail Bakhtin: The Dialogical Principle* (Minneapolis, MN: University of Minnesota Press, 1984).

TOEWS, John E.

1987. "Intellectual History after the Linguistic Turn: The Autonomy of Meaning and the Irreducibility of Experience", in the *American Historical Review* 82.4, 879–907.

1990? "The Historian in the Labyrinth of Signs: Reconstructing Cultures and Reading Texts in the Practise of Intellectual History", in *Semiotica* Special Issue on History, guest-edited by Brooke Williams and William Pencak (forthcoming).

TOULMIN, Stephen.
1982. "The Construal of Reality: Criticism in Modern and Postmodern Science", in *The Politics of Interpretation*, ed. W. J. T. Mitchell (Chicago, IL: University of Chicago Press).
von UEXKÜLL, Jakob.
1899–1940. *Kompositionslehre der Natur. Biologie als undogmatische Naturwissenschaft*, selected writings edited and with an introduction by T. von Uexküll (Frankfurt a. M.: Ullstein).
1920. *Theoretische Biologie* (Berlin; 2nd ed. 1928, reprinted Frankfurt a. M.: Suhrkamp 1970). Attempted English translation by MacKinnon 1926, q.v.
1934. *Streifzuge durch die Umwelten von Tieren und Menschen* (Berlin), trans. by Claire H. Schiller as "A Stroll through the Worlds of Animals and Men" in *Instinctive Behavior: The Development of a Modern Concept*, ed. by Claire H. Schiller (New York: International Universities Press, 1957), 5–80.
1940. "Bedeutungslehre", Bios 10 (Leipzig), trans. by Barry Stone and Herbert Weiner as "The Theory of Meaning" in *Semiotica* 42.1 (1982), 25–82.
von UEXKÜLL, Thure.
1981. "The Sign Theory of Jakob von Uexküll", in *Classics of Semiotics* (English edition of *Die Welt als Zeichen: Klassiker der modernen Semiotik*, Berlin: Wolf Jobst Siedler Verlag), ed. Martin Krampen, Klaus Oehler, Roland Posner, Thomas A. Sebeok, and Thure von Uexküll (New York: Plenum Press, 1987), 147–179.
1982. "Semiotics and the Problem of the Observer", in *Semiotics 1982*, ed. John Deely and Jonathan Evans (Lanham, MD: University Press of America, 1987), 3–12.
VERBEKE, G.
1978. "La Philosophie du Signe chez les Stoïciens", in *Les Stoiciens et Leur Logique*, ed. J. Brunschwig (Paris: Gallimard), 401–424.
VIVÈS, Ludovicus, ed.
1883–1886. The only complete modern edition (Paris), but based on the critically defective Lyons 1663 edition, of the 1637–1644 *Cursus Theologicus* of John Poinsot (discussion in Deely 1985: 396, 397, esp. 398 n. 3, 402 n. 7, 403 n. 8, 442, 459 n. 95); see Poinsot entry above.
VOLOŠINOV, V. N.
1926. "Slovo v zhini i slovo v poezii", *Zvezda* 6, 244–267, rendered "Discourse in Life and Discourse in Art (Concerning Sociological Poetics)" in *Freudianism: A Marxist Critique*, trans. and ed. by I. R. Titunik in collaboration with Neal H. Bruss (New York: Academic Press, 1976), 93–116, to which translation page references are keyed.
1929. *Marksism i filosofiia iazyka. Osnovnye problemy sotsiologicheskogo metoda v nauke o iazyke*, translated by Ladislav Matejka and I. R. Titunik as *Marxism and the Philosophy of Language* (New York: Seminar Press, 1973), to which translation page references are keyed.
WATT, W. C.
1984. "Signs of the Times" (review of De George 1981), *Semiotica* 50–1/2, 97–155.
WHEELER, John Archibald.
1984. "Bits, Quanta, Meaning", in *Problems in Theoretical Physics*, ed. A. Giovanni et al. (Salerno: University of Salerno Press), 121–141.
WILLIAMS, Brooke.
1982. "The Historian as Observer", in *Semiotics 1982*, ed. John Deely and Jonathan Evans (Lanham, MD: University Press of America, 1987), 13–25.

1983. "History as a Semiotic Anomaly", in *Semiotics 1983*, ed. Jonathan Evans and John Deely (Lanham, MD: University Press of America, 1987), 409–419.

1984. "Foreword" (Collingwood in Relation to Semiotic) to Russell 1984: vii-xx.

1985. "What Has History To Do with Semiotic?", *Semiotica* 54.1/2; preprinted in revised monograph form with index and historically layered bibliography under the title *History and Semiotic* (Victoria College of the University of Toronto: Toronto Semiotic Circle Number 4, Summer).

1985a. "Challenging Signs at the Crossroads", prefatory essay to Thomas A. Sebeok, *Contributions to the Doctrine of Signs* (= Sources in Semiotics IV; uncorrected reprint edition of 1976 original; Lanham, MD: University Press of America), xv-xlii.

1986. "History in Relation to Semiotic", reprint with modest revisions of 1983 above in Deely, Williams, and Kruse 1986: 217–223.

1987. "Introducing Semiotic to Historians", paper presented in the first AHA History and Semiotics session, at the One Hundred Second Annual Meeting of the American Historical Association, Washington, DC, 27–30 December 1987; available on microfilm or in xerographic form as part of the *Proceedings of the American Historical Association, 1987*, reference # 10485 (from: Order Fulfillment, University Microfilms International, 300 North Zeeb Road, Ann Arbor, MI 48106).

1987a. "Historiography as a Current Event", in *Semiotics 1987*, ed. John Deely (Lanham, MD: University Press of America, 1988), 479–486.

1988. "Opening Dialogue between the Discipline of History and Semiotics", in *The Semiotic Web: 1987*, ed. Thomas A. Sebeok and Donna Jean Umiker-Sebeok (Berlin: Mouton de Gruyter, 1988), 821–834.

WILLIAMS, Brooke, and William PENCAK, Guest-Editors.

1991. Special Issue of *Semiotica* on History, in press.

WINANCE, Eleuthère.

1983. Review article in *Revue Thomiste* LXXXIII, no. 3: 514–516.

Index

❏

JOHN DEELY, Professor and Chair of Philosophy at Loras College, is the design editor of the Annual Proceedings Volumes of the Semiotic Society of America, author of *Introducing Semiotic, The Tradition via Heidegger,* and *The Philosophical Dimensions of the Origin of Species,* translator and editor of *Tractatus de Signis: The Semiotic of John Poinsot,* co-editor (with Raymond J. Nogar) of *The Problem of Evolution,* and co-editor (with Brooke Williams and Felicia Kruse) of *Frontiers in Semiotics.*